'01

W9-CNM-443

Technical Analysis of the Currency Market

Founded in 1807, John Wiley & Sons is the oldest independent publishing company in the United States. With offices in North America, Europe, Australia, and Asia, Wiley is globally committed to developing and marketing print and electronic products and services for our customers' professional and personal knowledge and understanding.

The Wiley Trading series features books by traders who have survived the market's ever changing temperament and have prospered—some by reinventing systems, others by getting back to basics. Whether a novice trader, professional, or somewhere in-between, these books will provide the advice and strategies needed to prosper today and well into the future.

For a list of available titles, visit our web site at www.WileyFinance.com.

Technical Analysis of the Currency Market

*Classic Techniques
for Profiting from
Market Swings
and
Trader Sentiment*

BORIS SCHLOSSBERG

WILEY

John Wiley & Sons, Inc.

Copyright © 2006 by Boris Schlossberg. All rights reserved.

Published by John Wiley & Sons, Inc., Hoboken, New Jersey.
Published simultaneously in Canada.

No part of this publication may be reproduced, stored in a retrieval system, or transmitted in any form or by any means, electronic, mechanical, photocopying, recording, scanning, or otherwise, except as permitted under Section 107 or 108 of the 1976 United States Copyright Act, without either the prior written permission of the Publisher, or authorization through payment of the appropriate per-copy fee to the Copyright Clearance Center, Inc., 222 Rosewood Drive, Danvers, MA 01923, (978) 750-8400, fax (978) 646-8600, or on the web at www.copyright.com. Requests to the Publisher for permission should be addressed to the Permissions Department, John Wiley & Sons, Inc., 111 River Street, Hoboken, NJ 07030, (201) 748-6011, fax (201) 748-6008, or online at http://www.wiley.com/go/permissions.

Limit of Liability/Disclaimer of Warranty: While the publisher and author have used their best efforts in preparing this book, they make no representations or warranties with respect to the accuracy or completeness of the contents of this book and specifically disclaim any implied warranties of merchantability or fitness for a particular purpose. No warranty may be created or extended by sales representatives or written sales materials. The advice and strategies contained herein may not be suitable for your situation. You should consult with a professional where appropriate. Neither the publisher nor author shall be liable for any loss of profit or any other commercial damages, including but not limited to special, incidental, consequential, or other damages.

For general information on our other products and services or for technical support, please contact our Customer Care Department within the United States at (800) 762-2974, outside the United States at (317) 572-3993 or fax (317) 572-4002.

Wiley also publishes its books in a variety of electronic formats. Some content that appears in print may not be available in electronic books. For more information about Wiley products, visit our web site at www.wiley.com.

Library of Congress Cataloging-in-Publication Data:

Schlossberg, Boris.
    Technical analysis of the currency market : classic techniques for profiting
from market swings and trader sentiment / Boris Schlossberg.
        p.   cm.—(Wiley trading series)
    ISBN-13: 978-0-471-74593-8 (cloth)
    ISBN-10: 0-471-74593-6 (cloth)
    1. Foreign exchange futures.   2. Foreign exchange market.   3. Speculation.
I. Title.   II. Series.
HG3853.S35   2006
332.4'5—dc22
                                                            2005031905

Printed in the United States of America.

10   9   8   7   6   5   4   3   2   1

To my partner Kathy
without whom
none of this would be possible

Contents

Technical Analysis of the Currency Market

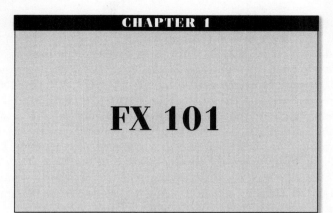

CHAPTER 1

FX 101

K now this. Technical analysis will not make you rich. It will not turn $1,000 into $1 million in a matter of weeks. It will not allow you to design a computer system that will automatically generate income while you luxuriate on the golf courses of Florida or snorkel in the azure blue waters of Cozumel.

Like every worthwhile endeavor in life, success in trading requires dedication, persistence, and a never-ending desire to excel. Technical analysis is only a tool—albeit a very good one—that if used properly can greatly sharpen and improve your trading in the currency market, but it cannot by itself make you a successful trader.

This book is about the practical application of technical analysis to the foreign exchange (FX or forex) markets. In it, I show you the key advantages as well as some of the limitations of this trading discipline. This book alone cannot guarantee success, but I can assure you of one thing: Your chances of winning will increase markedly if you learn to how to use technical analysis to trade FX.

Before turning to the business at hand, however, it's critical to understand how the FX market works and, more importantly, how it differs from all other financial markets that you may have traded.

TWO TRILLION REASONS TO TRADE

The FX market is the biggest financial market in the world. By the time you read this book its volume will have reached more than $2 trillion

1

per day in notional turnover. That's right—you didn't misread the numbers. The FX market trades 2 trillion with a T, not 2 billion with a B, dollars per day. Consider that the New York Stock Exchange (NYSE)—the biggest stock market in the world—processes only $60 billion worth of transactions on its busiest trading days of the year, and you can appreciate the scope and the size of the FX enterprise (see Figure 1.1).

Currency trading dwarfs all other markets in size, but it is a quiet giant of the finance field. Most financial media treat FX as an exotic afterthought rather than as the marquee financial market in the world. I am always amazed to flip open the finance section of the *Wall Street Journal* and see a tiny two-inch-square story buried deep on page C5 summarizing the day's action in the FX markets, while the front page of the finance section is entirely devoted to stocks and bonds.

Guess what? Though few investors realize this fact, the currency market has far more impact on the value of your overall investment portfolio than the quotidian events at Dell, General Motors (GM), or Wal-Mart. In a global economy, every major corporation is a multinational enterprise by necessity, and the direction of currencies can often affect these companies' profit margins more than any other input factor. Why do you think the FX market is so large? Because all of these multibillion-dollar corporations are its main customers.

- FX average daily volume of $2 trillion
- Volume has surged 57% over the past three years
- NYSE daily volume of $50 billion to $60 billion
- At least four times the size of the U.S. futures market

FIGURE 1.1   FX—A Growing Market

MARKET RULES

The only rule in the FX market is that there are no rules. Want to short with impunity to mercilessly drive down the value of the currency? Go right ahead. No artificial uptick sale rules will ever stop you. Your next-door neighbor's cousin overheard on the golf course that the Federal Reserve will announce a surprise rate hike next week? Feel free to empty out your bank account and load up on the trade. No one will come after you if you are proven right. In the FX market there is no such thing as insider trading. In fact, key European economic data such as German unemployment figures are often leaked to the press before their official release dates.

Suppose you are an institutional trader and a customer calls you to sell "one yard" ($1 billion worth) of euros in exchange for dollars right away. Suppose further that instead of executing the customer's order first, you decided to sell some EUR/USD from your firm's proprietary account, secure in the knowledge that the size of the customer's order will push the market lower by at least 15 points. Try that kind of front-running on the floor of the New York Stock Exchange or in the pits of the Chicago Mercantile Exchange (CME) and you'll wind up fined, unemployed, and possibly even jailed. In FX? No problem. You want to front-run customer order flow? Feel free to give it a try, but be warned you won't have those customers for long as they take their business to the hundreds of other market makers willing to provide fairer and more accurate execution.

While there is no global oversight for the FX market, there is very efficient self-regulation. Because key members both compete and depend on one another at the same time, any type of overt cheating is quickly eliminated as it poses tremendous structural danger to the market as a whole. You could say that in the case of FX "honor among thieves" works better than the iron fist of the regulators at ensuring that the market performs smoothly and efficiently.

Having said all that, I must note that FX is not the Wild West of finance, and in fact major money centers of the world do have regulatory agencies that oversee FX operations within their own jurisdictions. In the United States the FX market is overseen by the National Futures Association (NFA) and the Commodity Futures Trading Commission (CFTC). In the United Kingdom it is the Financial Service Authority (FSA) and in Japan it is the Ministry of Finance (MOF) that sets guidelines and regulations.

All of these regulators impose strict capital requirement rules for their member firms and audit their books on an annual or biannual basis. If the firm is regulated in the United States, you can see its net monthly capital statements (the amount of capital each firm possesses in excess of the minimum set by the regulators) at http://www.cftc.gov/tm/tmfcm.htm. You can also visit this webpage and see what, if any, complaints or regulatory actions have been lodged against the firm in the past.

For U.S.-based retail traders, doing business with a non-NFA member firm is like playing Russian roulette with your account. Not only will you not have any idea about the financial health of the dealer you trade with, but also you will have no real recourse if the company absconds with your money. However, any firm that is a member of the NFA must submit to binding arbitration in case of a dispute. So if you have an operational or a trade problem with the firm, there is a well-established legal procedure to adjudicate your grievances. Know this, however: While you have very important protection by dealing with an NFA-licensed firm, it, in turn, has no obligation to deal with you. That's right: If an FX dealer does not like the way you trade or the way you communicate with its dealing room or simply doesn't like your personality, it can ask you to wind up all your positions and close out your account. This, by the way, is true whether you are a small retail account from Toledo or a large hedge fund account from the Caribbean. In the FX market no one is obligated to do business with anyone else. In theory, Goldman Sachs could stop trading with Morgan Stanley, and Citibank could refuse to deal with Deutsche Bank. In practice, however, this almost never happens, but just as restaurants reserve the right to not serve certain patrons, dealers can refuse your business. The huge benefit of FX, of course, is that you can always find a dealer that may be more accommodative to your trading taste and style; just make sure that the firm is a member of the NFA.

MARKET STRUCTURE

Although in the past few years the popularity of FX has exploded among retail traders, the market is quite different from all other financial markets and still retains many of its old-boy network ways (see Figure 1.2).

The FX market trades 24 hours a day, 5 days per week, from about 5 P.M. eastern standard time on Sunday to 5 P.M. EST Friday afternoon. Trading kicks off in the sleepy capital of Wellington, New Zealand, moves over to Melbourne, Australia, and finally starts in earnest in Tokyo, Japan, which accounts for 15 percent of daily volume. At about 1 A.M. EST dealers arrive at their gunmetal desks in tall glass towers of Frankfurt, Germany, followed one hour later by colleagues in London, England, which, with more than 200 major dealing houses and fully 35 percent of average daily volume, represents the heart of the FX market. Finally, at 7 A.M. EST, bank dealers and hotshot hedge fund traders arrive at their desks on Wall Street and in Greenwich, Connecticut, and begin to deal

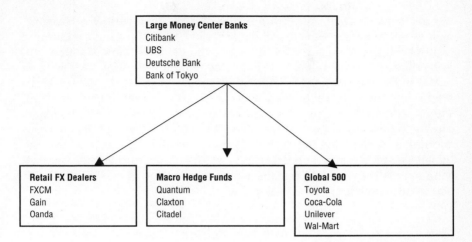

FIGURE 1.2 FX Market Structure

from their sleek multiple-panel-monitor computers, generating 25 percent of the day's volume.

At the core of the market are the primary dealers, including large money center banks such as Citibank and BankAmerica and global trading powerhouses like Goldman Sachs and Morgan Stanley. Slightly on the outside are the *Fortune* Global 2000 corporations—all the usual multinational names from Alcoa and Avantis to Wal-Mart and Unilever. Right behind them are the self-proclaimed masters of the universe—the huge, multibillion-dollar hedge funds (many of which are located in the downtowns of Stamford and Greenwich, Connecticut), which place massive leveraged bets on behalf of the world's most well-heeled investors while charging 2 percent of gross and 20 percent of profit for the privilege.

The market basically works like this: The big money center banks like Citibank, Bank of Tokyo, and Deutsche Bank, along with trading houses like Goldman Sachs, Morgan Stanley, and UBS, act as primary market makers supplying liquidity to the market. They are linked to each other and to the outside world through banks of phones and Reuters and EBS terminals. Although in the past most dealing was conducted by phone, now many billion-dollar trades are settled through screen-based trading with a click of a mouse.

The multinational corporations are the primary hedgers in the market looking to offset their business risk—everything from import and export costs to such mundane matters as weekly payroll management. The hedge funds are the large speculators looking to profit from changes in major economic and political trends. Last but certainly not least are the world's central banks, which participate in the market for a variety of reasons. Some central banks come into the market just to balance their books and adjust their foreign reserves. Others, like the People's Bank of China, will sometimes day trade billions of dollars at a clip if they think they have an edge, and will often pocket millions of dollars in profit for their reserve vaults. Yet other central banks will come into the market to try to manipulate or defend their country's currency to protect their trade advantage. How committed are they to this task? In 2003 the Bank of Japan spent more than $300 billion in a matter of a few months to make sure that the Japanese yen remained cheap relative to the dollar so that the country's vital export sector could remain competitive on the global stage. In FX, the game is definitely played for keeps.

DECENTRALIZATION

There is no central governing authority that controls trading. There is no central FX exchange. There is no single clearinghouse. Business in the biggest market in the world is basically done on a handshake. If you trade stocks, all of the transactions are settled though a central exchange like the NYSE or NASDAQ; if you trade futures, the CME or the Chicago Board of Trade (CBOT) makes sure that your trades are cleared. It's the same in options, where the two biggest players, the Chicago Board of Trade (CBOE) and ISE (pronounced "ice" on Wall Street), stand to settle your trades. The exchanges' main function is to guarantee that disparate groups of buyers and sellers can come together and make trades without having to worry about whether the guy on the other side is good for the money.

Not so in FX. FX is known as the party-to-party market. You deal directly with your market maker and there is no third party guaranteeing the transaction. Everybody works with everybody else on a credit basis. That essentially means that everybody must trust each other to settle up. Settlement, by the way, is two business days forward, but of course due to modern technology every player in the market knows their true exposure in real time.

Decentralization makes the FX market unique. Unlike exchange-based stock or bond markets, there is no central order book and there is no best bid or offer price. In fact, in FX there is no single price for a given currency at any one time. Just like in a Middle Eastern bazaar where prices for identical Persian rugs may differ from one merchant's stall to the next, so too in FX prices for EUR/USD may vary depending on which dealer's quote you receive. This process may seem bewildering and arcane, but the wide array of participants actually makes the FX market the most efficient and liquid in the world. In reality, competition among market makers is so fierce that the bid/ask difference in the the EUR/USD— the most active financial instrument in the world—is often only 1 point wide, equivalent to only 0.01 percent of the contract value.

BASIC QUOTATION CONVENTION

In FX, currencies are quoted to four decimal points. Whereas in real life products are priced to the penny, so a pack of gum, for instance, will cost you $1.25, in FX the quotation is extended to one-hundredth of a penny. The same hypothetical pack of gum will be quoted at $1.2500 bid/$1.2503 asked. A daily move of one penny is considered a large move in the FX market, and since each point is worth one-hundredth of a penny, that translates to a 100-point gain or loss depending on which side of the market you find yourself on.

A point in FX is called a pip—an acronym for "percentage in point"— and is essentially equal to one basis point. Currencies are always quoted in pairs, like EUR/USD for example. The first part of the pair, in this case the euro, is called the base currency, and the second part, in this case the dollar, is called the countercurrency. Contract size in the institutional interbank market is standardized at 1 million units of currency. In the retail FX market, standard contracts are 100,000 units in size. However, all retail dealers offer mini-contracts of only 10,000 units, and many also offer even smaller contracts of 1,000 units (micro lot) or even 100 currency units (hundred lot). Because pip values are determined by the countercurrency, pairs such as EUR/USD that have the U.S. dollar at the end of the quote are easy to price. Since each pip is one-hundredth of 1 percent, it is worth $10 on a 100,000-unit contract, $1 on a 10,000-unit mini-contract, 1 dime on a 1,000-unit contract, and 1 penny on a 100-unit contract.

Pairs that have a currency other than the dollar as the countercurrency, such as USD/CHF (dollar/Swiss franc), for example, require a little work to figure out. Essentially, you have to obtain the present market value of the currency in terms of dollars and then multiply it by the contract value. Let's say the Swiss franc is worth 0.8 U.S. dollars. Then in the case of USD/CHF a pip value is worth $8.00 on a 100,000-unit contract, 80 cents on a 10,000-unit contract, 8 cents on a 1,000-unit contract, and only 0.8 pennies on a 100-unit contract (see Table 1.1).

One of the greatest aspects of the FX market is that your cost of doing business will always be proportionately the same regardless of what size you trade. This is a huge difference from all other markets, where the

TABLE 1.1 Value of Pips in Pairs Where the Dollar Is
the Countercurrency

Contract	Size in Currency Units	Pip Value
Standard Lot	100,000 units	$10.00
Mini Lot	10,000 units	$ 1.00
Micro Lot	1,000 units	$ 0.10
Hundred Lot	100 units	$ 0.01

smallest trader usually pays the highest proportionate cost. In stocks, for example, a trader who places a 10,000-share trade of a $1 stock may be charged only $10 to buy and $10 to sell the security, making the trader's effective cost of doing business about 0.2 percent, but the same trader placing only a 100-share order will likely be charged the same $10 minimum both ways, making the effective cost of doing business 20 percent! Not so in FX. The cost of doing business whether you choose to trade 1 million units or 100 units of currency is usually between three-hundredths and 10-hundredths of 1 percent, allowing even the smallest speculator in Peoria to go toe-to-toe against a billion-dollar trader in London on totally equal terms.

DEALING VERSUS BROKERING: NO SCALPING ALLOWED

For the retail trader, FX offers an almost intoxicating degree of freedom. You can trade 24 hours a day, 5 days a week (from about 5 P.M. EST Sunday to 5 P.M. EST Friday afternoon). All you need is an Internet connection and your dealer's trading platform. Some dealers require that you download their software, while others simply let you trade through the browser. You can trade with as little as $300 or as much as $30 million in capital for the exact same cost because the market charges no commissions. That's right—traders do not pay commissions in FX, because this is a dealer-based market. Instead of using a broker who charges a commission to take the order to an exchange to be executed by a market maker, traders in FX deal directly with the market maker and simply buy on the offer and sell at the bid. There are no additional fees—no Securities and Exchange Commission (SEC) charges, no exchange access fees, nothing more. Once traders clear the difference between the bid/ask spread, every penny gain thereafter is their own.

Although there are no commissions in the market, there is, of course, a cost to doing business. That cost is the bid/ask spread, and this is perhaps the most important point to absorb about the FX market. Unlike in stocks, futures, options, and all other exchange-traded instruments, traders are unable to buy on the bid or sell on the ask. In FX, trading is conducted directly with the market maker, so traders cannot assume the role of the market maker themselves.

For traders who are used to making hundreds of tiny day trades on the electronic exchange markets of today, this aspect of the FX market can be a huge adjustment because it means traders cannot effectively scalp the market. Scalping, the art of buying at the bid and quickly selling at the offer or a few ticks higher, becomes almost futile mathematically. Using the absolute best example of EUR/USD, the most liquid currency pair in the world, we can see just how difficult it is. The spread in the EUR/USD is typically 2 to 3 points wide. If traders are scalping for a very modest target of 10 points using a 1:1 reward-to-risk ratio (i.e., they are willing to risk 10 points to make 10 points), their actual reward-to-risk ratio would be considerably worse. They would need to earn 13 points to make a 10-point profit (10 + 3 points for the spread). Conversely, they could not lose more than 7 points (10 − 3 points of spread).

More importantly, most dealers do not like scalpers, whom they essentially view as little more than thieves trying to steal their profits from the spread. They reserve special dislike for traders whom they deem "pickers." These are traders who have accounts with many different retail FX firms and may even have access to the interbank prices disseminated through the EBS system. Because of the decentralized nature of the market, the price feeds of some of the retail dealers may momentarily lag the market. Pickers essentially look for these discrepancies and try to take advantage of the mispricing by hitting the late feeds, which they resell for a quick profit back to the dealers as their price feeds catch up to the general market. To an outside observer this activity may appear as nothing more than plain-vanilla arbitrage, but one person's arbitrage is another person's theft. In a spread-based market, dealers get very cross with traders who try to muscle in on their primary means of earning a profit and will eventually put such traders on manual execution—a process known as dealer intervention. Traders put on dealer intervention must have all of their trades confirmed by the dealer rather than have them instantly executed through electronic dealing. Although in practice the process delays execution by no more than 15 seconds, for traders who are accustomed to harvesting profits from short-term changes in momentum this can be a fate worse than death. They will no doubt experience subpar execution and will suffer substantial slippage costs as dealers may in effect "freeze the clock" on them.

Is this fair? Most retail traders used to the bid/ask access of electronic stock, futures, and options markets will surely say no. If your game plan involves making up to 200 round trip trades for 1 to 5 points each in a matter of five to six hours, then FX may not be the market for you unless you are willing to change your approach. You have to make a sobering comparison between the advantages of all-electronic markets that allow you to have the possibility of buying at the bid and selling at the ask, but charge a commission in the process, against the FX market, which forbids bid/ask access but charges no commission fees. Before you jump to conclusions, I urge you to consult your end-of-year broker-age statements. Each trader is clearly different but I know that in my case of very active trading in the electronic futures markets my broker often made three times more in commissions versus what I earned in capital gains. When comparing costs of trading in this manner, the FX market can actually appear to be quite reasonable.

LEVERAGE AND CUSTOMIZATION

If you trade stocks, the standard leverage is 2:1. That is, you need to put up $50 of cash or marketable securities (called margin) in order to purchase $100 worth of stock. If you have more than $25,000 in your account you qual-ify for day trading rules and can increase your leverage to 4:1. In either case you will have to pay interest on the amount of money you borrow at what-ever loan rate your broker charges you on your margin. During the Internet bubble era of 1998–2000 some major Wall Street wire houses made more money on their margin loan business than on brokering commissions. In fact, much like a Las Vegas casino that provides free drinks as long as you stay and gamble on the casino floor, these wire houses could have let their customers trade commission free as long as they margined their accounts.

Moving on to options, the leverage increases 10:1. If you are an option buyer the cost of your trade is limited to the premium paid, and no inter-est is charged. In futures, leverage increases to 20:1; in other words, a trader needs to place only $5 to control $100 worth of futures contracts. Furthermore, as collateral the trader can put up Treasury bills and effec-tively receive interest while staying in the trade.

In FX leverage is taken to a whole different level. Standard leverage in FX is typically 100:1, meaning that you need to put down only 1 per-cent of the face value of the contract. However, many dealers offer 200:1 leverage, and some even extend credit on a 400:1 basis. At 400:1 leverage a trader in essence can use a quarter to control $100 worth of currency. Is that insane? Yes and no. The question of leverage is a personal prefer-ence and depends on your answer to the question of how much risk you want to take.

Some people like to drive fast, while some people like to drive slow.

At 400:1 leverage a trader is engaging in the same activity as a driver who flies down the interstate at 150 miles per hour. The thrill is certainly great and so is the speediness of the trip, but even the smallest pebble, the tiniest swerve, or a minimal slowdown ahead can result in instant death. Fortunately, the consequences in FX are not that drastic. The only death traders can experience is that of their capital being consumed by the market.

Yet for many traders the high leverage of FX holds a special appeal. Not only can the trader control a huge position with very little money (at 400:1 leverage $2,500 of margin can control $1 million worth of EUR/USD, for example) but the 24-hour nature of currency trading provides traders with protection found in no other market.

MARGIN CALL

Almost everyone who has traded financial products on a leveraged basis has faced a margin call at least once. A margin call is simply a request from your broker for more funds when the value of your collateral for your trade declines below minimum requirements. That of course sounds so civilized, but in real life it is in fact the financial equivalent of a desperate cry for more money. If you accede to the demand and the trade continues to move against you, this dynamic begins to resemble a black hole as your capital becomes mercilessly absorbed by the market. But if you choose to ignore the margin call, you broker will automatically close out your position, likely for a huge loss, in a process known as forced liquidation. One of the reasons this process is so painful is that it forces traders to liquidate their positions not on terms of their own choosing but on the terms of their broker. Quite often margin calls take traders out of their positions right at the bottom or top of the move—thus denying them the chance to allow the trades to recover.

Yet that is not the worst aspect of the margin call. In exchange-based markets that are open only during set business hours, traders are always in danger of suffering hugely adverse moves because of gaps in price at the open. In fact, though few traders realize it, their financial risk can be far greater than just the money in their accounts. In futures markets especially, where bad weather or geopolitical unrest can cause several days' worth of limit up or limit down moves when price movement is capped by predetermined rules, many speculators have lost not only their accounts but their whole net worth after having to meet massive margin calls from their brokers.

FX is different. Because markets are open 24 hours a day, dealers can always find liquidity and therefore offer guarantees to traders that they will never lose more money than they put into their accounts. To be sure, margin calls in FX are automatic—there are no circumspect calls from account executives asking for money or even informing the trader of the fact of the margin call trigger. The dealer's risk management software simply closes out all positions the second they breach margin levels as machines perform the task with brutal efficiency. But the advantage is that traders can sleep soundly knowing that their risk is strictly limited.

It is because of this unique feature of the FX market that some traders like to utilize the extreme leverage offered by the market makers. For these traders, the high leverage and the automatic margin call feature turn the FX trading into a de facto option contract on steroids. Imagine the following. You are a retail trader who has allocated $10,000 for speculative capital. However, instead of putting all $10,000 into your FX account you deposit only $1,000 and keep the other $9,000 in your bank account. At 400:1 leverage you can control up to 400,000 units of currency with just this $1,000 deposit. However, under those circumstances even a 1-point move against your position would trigger a margin call, so instead you decide to trade a maximum of 200,000 or two standard lots. With margin set at $250 per lot you will have $500 of available margin for your position:

    $1,000 initial deposit
    – $500 margin requirement ($250 × 2 lots = $500)
    = $500/2 lots = $250 or 25 points of risk

In other words, you have just created a position that acts very much like a long option trade; that is, your upside is uncapped while your risk is limited to capital invested. In reality the risk is even less, since presumably your position would be liquidated with $500 still in the account minus any slippage that may occur. Even better than a real-life option, the position has no expiration date and its delta is 1, meaning that you will participate in any profitable move point for point with price.

Thus, while leverage is clearly dangerous, this particular strategy of judiciously deploying only controlled portions of your speculative capital may work quite well for aggressive traders who like to maximize their trades. After all, going back to our initial example, if the trader was correct on direction and EUR/USD moved 200 points his way, he would be able to bank $4,000 of profit (200 points × 2 standard lots at $10 per point) on risk of little more than $500. Unfortunately, most novice traders do not trade like that. They will instead put all of their speculative capital into their account at the highest leverage possible, take a trade that goes against them without leaving any stop-loss orders, and then watch helplessly as their position is finally liquidated with less than a quarter of their capital left.

High leverage presents yet another problem—it leaves the trader with very little room to maneuver. The higher the leverage, the smaller the margin for error. Even in our previous example where you, the trader, use only a small portion of your overall capital, your biggest possible drawdown before margin call liquidation kicks in is only 25 points. Given the fact that the average daily range in EUR/USD can exceed 100 points, you can easily be stopped out of a trade that could eventually move your way. That's why many successful traders use the opposite approach. Taking advantage of mini or even micro lots, they trade with a very small leverage factor and instead scale into trades over large price ranges in order to avoid frequent stop-outs and achieve a blended price closer to actual market price.

LEARN THE CARRY OR PAY THE PRICE

Regardless of how it is used, leverage is a critical aspect of currency trading that leads us to a discussion of the most common trading strategy in the market—the carry trade. In FX every currency carries an interest rate. These interest rates are set by the central banks of their respective countries, and within the industrialized world can vary widely (see Figure 1.3). In 2005, for example, one of the largest interest rate differentials existed between Australia and Japan. The Australian economy, buoyed by a huge demand from China for metals and commodities, has experienced strong growth at the beginning of the new century, with unemployment reaching

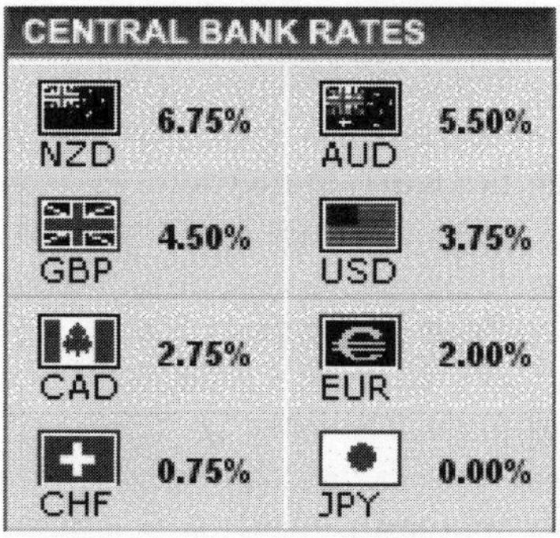

CENTRAL BANK RATES			
NZD	6.75%	AUD	5.50%
GBP	4.50%	USD	3.75%
CAD	2.75%	EUR	2.00%
CHF	0.75%	JPY	0.00%

FIGURE 1.3 Central Bank Rates
Source: DailyFX (www.dailyfx.com).

all-time lows and the housing market booming. In order to control growth, the Reserve Bank of Australia steadily increased interest rates until by 2005 they reached 5.50 percent. Meanwhile, Japan's central bank, trying to revive the country's economy after its decade long bout with deflation, maintained an ultra-accommodative monetary policy, setting interest rates at 0 percent. Thus the spread between the two interest rates was 5.50 percent, establishing the groundwork for the carry trade—the most popular FX strategy among the multibillion-dollar hedge funds.

The premise of the carry trade is simple. A trader goes long the currency with the higher yield and short the currency with the lower yield. In the case of the AUD/JPY trade, the trader would receive 5.50 percent annual interest on his long Aussie dollar position while being obligated to pay nothing on his short yen position because JPY interest rates were 0 percent. The net spread on the trade would be 5.50 percent. If the price of AUD/JPY did not change by even 1 point from the time of the trade to one year forward, the trader would still be able to harvest 5.50 percent in profit from interest income alone.

While a 5.50 percent annual rate of return may seem only mildly interesting, the true power of the carry trade comes from leverage. The very same trader on only 10:1 leverage would now earn 55 percent per year, even if the currency pair remained completely stationary. If the trade also generated capital appreciation of 5 percent or more, on 10:1 leverage returns could jump to triple digits!

The carry trade explains the principal dynamic behind hedge funds' outsized compensation schedule, which typically translates to 2 percent of gross assets and 20 percent of net profits. Yet the principles of the strategy are extremely simple, and some may wonder just why these masters of the universe are so well paid. Whatever the reasons, the key question is: Why is the carry trade important to the technically oriented trader? For traders who intend only to day trade and close out all their positions by 5 P.M. EST (the official close of the trading day in FX), the answer is that it is not important at all. However, for any swing or longer-term trader, ignorance of the carry trade can be an expensive lesson to learn. Note that traders who are on the positive side of the carry will receive an interest credit into their accounts every single day. However, traders who are short the carry trade will have interest deducted from their accounts every day. On currency pairs with large differentials the cost per day can quickly add up. Consider the GBP/JPY pairing, which at the time of writing (summer of 2005) had a differential of 475 basis points. Every day a trader who was short the pair would be debited 2.5 points (or approximately $25). That may not sound like much, but note that at 100:1 the trader would need to put down only $1,000 to control 100,000 units of GBP/JPY, and after only 10 days fully one-quarter ($250) of his margin would be eaten away by the carry trade costs. Imagine the trade lasting 1,001 days during which the trader would pay $2,500 in interest rate costs, fully 2.5 times his minimal required margin! Now perhaps you can appreciate why even the most technically oriented trader needs to know about the carry trade. In FX the dictum is: Learn the carry or pay the price.

In FX even many traders who are pure technicians will not trade against the carry. Yet trading in the opposite direction of the carry can be very profitable as well. Currencies with the widest differentials in interest rates often have the highest-volatility moves. For traders who thrive on volatility this is a tremendous gift. Using tools and techniques that I will show you, you will be able to better time your entries and possibly capture the huge swings in price that result from many speculators exiting the carry trade all at once. However, the key rule about countertrading the carry trade that nobody should ever forget is: Be right or be out.

A few final warnings about practices to watch out for: The carry trade interest is paid at the discretion of the dealer, but carry trade interest costs are *always* charged. Before opening an account with a dealer, always ask what the rules of the house are. Some dealers are terrifically forthright and will pay you interest on any amount of capital you may have on deposit and will even compound it for you hourly. Other dealers will ask that you trade on 2 percent margin or higher but will offer some of the highest carry credits in the business. Yet other less-scrupulous dealers will not pay any credits on the carry and will charge interest on countercarry positions. Finally, the absolutely worst dealers may offer a smattering of interest credit but will charge upwards of 300 percent of actually carry costs for anyone trading the countercarry position. To translate that into actual numbers, if the true carry cost on GBP/JPY is about 2.5 points or $25 per day, these dealers may charge 7.5 points or $75 per day, turning what is essentially a common financial service in the FX world into a surreptitious profit center for the firm.

How do they get away with it? Ignorance. Many traders are not even aware of the interest rate dynamics of currencies that underlie the carry trade. These novice speculators blissfully trade away their capital without even realizing they are being fleeced.

GOOD TECHNICIANS KNOW THEIR FUNDAMENTALS

Can you trade FX from price charts only? Yes, but that would like fighting with one arm tied behind your back. FX is a news-driven market, and basic awareness of fundamentals is tremendously helpful to your success as a trader. You may find it amusing that a book on technical analysis is espousing the value of fundamental data, but having a clear idea as to what fundamental factors matter to the market helps the technical trader to properly assess the technical picture. Just as the gastroenterologist will want to know what you've recently eaten so that she may analyze the results of an upper gastrointestinal tract exam in proper context, so, too, a technician will be able to draw more accurate conclusions from price patterns if he knows and understands the impact of economic news. Many technicians like to dismiss fundamental data on the grounds that it is often complex and contradictory and that currencies will frequently react in the exact opposite way from what fundamental data would indicate. This is certainly true, and doubly so for the day-to-day economic releases, which can muddy short-term trading with volatile swings up and down. However, major economic news is vital to understanding and succeeding in the market. Understand the story and you will understand your trade. It is far easier to hold a technical position on both emotional and intellectual grounds if the fundamental picture supports your position.

Bruce Kovner, one of the largest and most seasoned currency speculators in the world, a man so good that other traders give him their retirement funds to manage, summed it up best in Jack D. Schwager's seminal book, *Market Wizards* (New York Institute of Finance, 1989; HarperBusiness, 1993). When asked by Schwager what he thought was more important, fundamental or technical analysis, Kovner replied, "This is like asking a doctor whether he would prefer treating a patient with diagnostics or with a chart monitoring his condition. You need both."

Technical traders who trade price only, so as not to be confused by the news, are simply being lazy in their decision-making process. Price does not form in a vacuum, and a trader who is ignorant of fundamental news will not be able to adjust to or profit from the changing tone of the market. As we'll see later on, indicators that work great in one environment fail miserably in another; the key difference between success and failure is understanding which trading regime the market is in and adapting accordingly. Truly great technical traders are always aware of the news backdrop and know how to exploit it with technical tools.

Although the array of economic data released into the markets by various government agencies on a daily basis can be staggering—and it is easy to understand how some traders can feel overwhelmed—understanding fundamental data in the currency markets is really quite simple. No advanced degrees in macroeconomics are required—really. Four key themes drive the currency markets:

1. Economic growth
2. Interest rates

3. Trade balance
4. Political stability

Economic Growth

An expanding gross domestic product (GDP) will take care of a multitude of sins. The most basic and fundamental fact that FX markets like to focus on is the strength of economic activity. Much like individual company earnings, the country's gross domestic product measures the basic health of the economy. If GDP is expanding rapidly—and most importantly if that growth takes place in a noninflationary environment—the currency market will most likely bid up the currency due to investors' desire to participate in this positive story.

Interest Rates

This factor relates directly to our friend the carry trader. Typically, when economic growth picks up, the country's central bank will begin to increase interest rates in order to prevent too much speculative activity in the economy from creating imbalances and inflation. As interest rates increase, carry traders flock to the currency and bid up its value. The one exception to this scenario is if the central bank raises rates not as a policy response to rapid growth but as a means of curtailing runaway inflation. Such circumstances would suggest that the country is awash in too much money stock, and the FX market would therefore be wary of bidding up the currency regardless of what interest rate was attached, as the fear of further debasement of the currency would outweigh the reward of a higher yield. A good way to understand why that happens is to imagine the following situation.

Suppose your next-door neighbor asks to borrow $1,000 for a month and is willing to pay you 10 percent in interest for the privilege. You've known the man for 20 years. He has always been honest and honorable in his dealings and you also know that he has run a successful business for the past 10 years. Would you take the risk of lending him money for a month? Most likely yes. Now imagine you are approached by a man on the street you do not know. His hair is matted, his fingernails are dirty, and unfortunately his arm displays the unmistakable scars of a heroin junkie. The man asks you for a $100 loan payable in one day with 100 percent interest. Would you loan this fellow the money? You may give him money as charity, but if your decision were based strictly on business reasons, clearly the answer would be no. Although his promised rate of interest is 10 times the size of your neighbor's, his lack of creditworthiness outweighs the potential rewards.

Much in the same way, a high interest rate in a currency does not guarantee appreciation if it's a result of high inflation rather than strong economic growth.

Trade Balance

The flow of goods and services between two countries can have a tremendous effect on currency movements. The idea is really quite simple. Imagine two countries. Country A sells $100 billion more products to Country B than it buys. In order to purchase those goods and services, citizens of Country B have to buy Country A's currency and sell their own. Thus Country A—the country with a trade surplus—will have an appreciating currency, and Country B—the country with the trade deficit—will see its currency decline.

This is, of course, an extremely simplified example. In the real world trade balance issues can become quite complicated. Honda's plants in Martinsville, Ohio, actually *export* some of their vehicles back to Japan, while the United States can pay for its deficits by simply printing more dollars, because the dollar is the reserve currency in FX. Nevertheless, this basic model is critical to understanding the valuation of currencies and can help the trader grasp why currencies decline in value when their trade balance deficits become too large.

Political Stability

If you are a political junkie, the FX market is truly your domain. Unlike the stock market, where it doesn't matter if the U.S. President comes from a red state or a blue state as long as your portfolio is green, in FX politics can have a massive impact. After all, we are trading the fates of nations, not companies, so political as well as economic concerns will influence the market. Even if politics is not your bailiwick, it is very important to understand that the FX market hates political instability because it then cannot rationally handicap future economic growth. That's why countries with strong economic growth will often see their currencies decline if there is even a hint of political upheaval, especially if it involves any sort of corruption within the government. A good example of such a dynamic happened in the summer of 2005 when the Canadian dollar experienced a bout of weakness against the U.S. dollar despite rising oil prices, which were highly beneficial to energy-rich Canada. The reason? Worries over the stability of the ruling Liberal Party government led by Paul Martin, which was embroiled in a political scandal. As soon as Paul Martin survived the no-confidence motion (by one vote, mind you) the Canadian dollar regained its strength.

For technically oriented traders, keeping an eye on these four simple fundamental factors can provide a far better and richer perspective for making successful trades. In fact, just as divergence is one of the key tools in technical trading, so it can be in fundamental trading as well. In 2004 when the U.S. dollar was making all-time lows against the euro, the U.S. economy was actually producing a string of consistent positive economic surprises. Astute technical traders who tracked this data shorted the euro with a great degree of confidence once their technical tools signaled price weakness and were able to stay in the trade as the dollar's fortunes turned in 2005.

TRY BEFORE YOU BUY

One very underappreciated benefit of retail FX is that every dealer offers a free demo trading account that allows the trader to experiment with the trading platform before actually risking any capital. The demo accounts are exact replicas of the dealer's real trading platforms. The dealer simply funds the account with "demo dollars" in amounts ranging from $5,000 to $100,000 and allows the trader to trade to his heart's content. Some demo accounts automatically expire after 30 days, while others can live in perpetuity. Regardless of the specifics, they are all valuable because they allow traders to test not only their strategies but also the execution capabilities of the platform. Since FX is a decentralized market, each platform is unique. Some have advanced charting, back-testing capabilities, and the latest FX news all built in. Others are simply stripped-down execution engines with all the glamour of a Soviet-style factory.

Don't be fooled, however, by pretty candles and fancy indicators. The key value of a sound FX platform is speed and accuracy of execution. It does a trader little good to have beautiful charts and highly profitable back-tested strategies if the dealer cannot provide a smooth and consistent price feed. By watching the demo, a trader can also learn how each dealer makes its spreads. Does the dealer always keep spreads fixed? Or do spreads widen out in times of high volatility? Dealer A may keep spreads in EUR/USD 2 pips wide, while Dealer B's spreads are 3 pips wide. However, during major news releases like nonfarm payrolls Dealer A may widen spreads to 20 pip, meaning that the currency would have to move 20 points in the trader's direction before he could break even on the position. Dealer B may keep spreads fixed at 3 pips regardless of market volatility. Which dealer is better? The answer depends a lot on your trading style. However, if you are a short-term trader, wide spreads could negatively affect profitability.

Another key factor in comparing dealing platforms is determining what amount of currency can be traded in the account. Some dealers only allow traders to execute mini (10,000-unit) and standard (100,000-unit) lots. Many even require a separate account for each size the trader wishes to trade. Other brokers, in contrast, allow traders to make trades as small as 1 unit to as large as 10 million units all from one platform. (Yes, you could actually buy and sell 1 unit of currency on some platforms! In the case of EUR/USD, if the pair went your way for 1,000 points you would make a whopping 10 cents on your trade.) Somewhere in the middle are dealers who will allow trades in increments of 1,000 units or larger. Again, the importance of small size capability depends on the trader. If you scale into your positions in many small increments, then small lots are a must. If, however, you are a single entry/single exit trader, "flexi-lots" are not nearly as important.

Yet another key fact to ascertain beforehand is how various dealers charge and credit interest on your positions. Every dealer will charge interest, but some will not credit it. Others will credit interest but only if the account is first set to a margin of 2 percent or higher. Still others will simply not credit interest as a matter of policy. Even worse, some dealers will charge interest as high as three times the actual market rate while offering credit at below market rate. In contrast, other dealers will calculate and credit interest on an hourly rather than daily basis and require no account or margin minimums. A decentralized market has decentralized rules. By trading the demo, traders will discover the quirks before they can impact their working capital. How important are these differences in interest payment policy? If the trader trades only short-term, closing all positions every day before the 5 P.M. EST rollover time, they are meaningless. However, if carry trading is a large part of the trader's strategy or he is simply a position trader, dealer interest policy is crucial.

One area that gets completely overlooked by traders because it is so mundane is the reporting capability of the each platform. Granted, account reporting is hardly the first concern of an FX speculator—but in many cases it should be. Understand that in case of an active trader who places 10 trades per day, an end-of-year statement can generate 2,500 entries. Some dealers' platforms have terrifically sophisticated reporting capabilities that segregate every single position, separate interest payments and credits, and summarize the end-of-year equity position in a simple, easy-to-understand format that can literally be handed to the accountant and mailed to the Internal Revenue Service (IRS) with almost no additional work. Other platforms will spit out such confusing mishmash that traders may have to spend hundreds of hours of preparation reconciling their trades before they can conform to generally accepted accounting principles (GAAP). Again, trading the demo allows the trader to test the reporting capabilities of the platform to determine whether they are an asset or a liability (see Tables 1.2 through 1.4). Note how this

Ticket #	Currency	Volume	Date	Sold	Bought	Gross P/L
02362313	GBP/CHF	300K	1/8/04 3:13 PM		2.2483	
			1/19/04 11:07 AM	2.2600		2,769.12
02366530	AUD/CAD	300K	1/13/04 9:41 AM		0.9935	
			1/19/04 12:14 PM	0.9797		-3,182.78
02367875	AUD/NZD	300K	1/14/04 10:51 AM		1.1395	
			2/2/04 6:35 AM	1.1300		-1,913.35
02370237	USD/CHF	200K	1/20/04 8:43 AM	1.2550		
			1/23/04 2:32 AM		1.2300	4,065.04
02370388	USD/CHF	200K	1/20/04 8:43 AM	1.2550		
			1/26/04 1:43 PM		1.2550	0.00

TABLE 1.2 Closed Trade List
Source: Forex Capital Markets (FXCM).

Order #	Type	Ticket	Currency	Volume	Date	B/S
09472459	S	04477094	EUR/GBP	100K	7/13/05 6:09 PM	S
09493837	S	04487134	USD/CAD	100K	7/18/05 6:27 PM	B
09493839	S	04487149	USD/CAD	100K	7/18/05 6:27 PM	B
09498497	LE	04489229	USD/CAD	100K	7/19/05 10:05 AM	B
09508811	S	04493888	EUR/GBP	100K	7/20/05 6:51 PM	S
09517404	LE	04497858	GBP/USD	100K	7/21/05 4:48 PM	S
	S				7/21/05 4:48 PM	B

TABLE 1.3 Outstanding Orders
Source: Forex Capital Markets (FXCM).

Ticket #	Currency	Volume	Date	Sold	Bought	Floating P/L	Comm
04477094	EUR/GBP	100K	7/13/05 6:09 PM		0.6853	1,477.26	0.00
			7/23/05 2:39 PM	0.6938			
04487134	USD/CAD	100K	7/18/05 6:24 PM	1.2177		-106.64	0.00
			7/23/05 2:39 PM		1.2190		
04487149	USD/CAD	100K	7/19/05 8:52 AM	1.2220		246.10	0.00
			7/23/05 2:39 PM		1.2190		
04493888	EUR/GBP	100K	7/20/05 6:51 PM		0.6988	-868.98	0.00
			7/23/05 2:39 PM	0.6938			
Total:						747.74	0.00
Posted at statement period of time:							0.00

TABLE 1.4 Open/Floating Positions
Source: Forex Capital Markets (FXCM).

platform elegantly separates closed trades, outstanding orders, and floating positions and then tidily summarizes all the key activity in the account summary (see Table 1.5).

This platform shows only transaction history, though, leaving traders to their own devices to reconcile transactions by trade. Some platforms provide a trade history listing each transaction (see Table 1.6).

However, the question of whether the platform executes well during times of stress is impossible to answer on the demo platform, as the demo platforms are often assigned to a different set of servers and may perform flawlessly, while the real account servers could experience blackouts due to overwhelming volume.

	Beginning Balance	0.00
Comm	Trading Commission	0.00
Intr	Interest Fee	8,642.42
PnL	Profit/Loss of Trade	−37,036.95
Depos	Deposit	515,174.66
Withd	Withdrawal	−408,977.37
Option	Options Payout	0.00
Comm	Options Commission	0.00
WithdFee	Withdrawal Fee	0.00
MngFee	Management Fee	0.00
PerfFee	Performance Fee	0.00
	Ending Balance	77,802.76
	Floating P/L	747.74
	Equity	**78,550.50**
	Necessary Margin	8,000.00
	Usable Margin	70,550.50

TABLE 1.5 Account Summary
Source: Forex Capital Markets (FXCM).

Click on an arrow or the title link to sort the columns of the table.

DATE	TICKET	TICKET LINK	TYPE	PAIR	UNITS	PRICE	AMOUNT	Account Balance
Fri Jan 14 14:47:06 2005	36930761		AddFunds	USD		0	500.0000	500.00
Fri Jan 14 16:00:00 2005	36948410		Interest	USD		0	0.0264	500.03
Sat Jan 15 16:00:00 2005	36964941		Interest	USD		0	0.0274	500.05
Sun Jan 16 16:00:00 2005	36981636		Interest	USD		0	0.0274	500.08
Sun Jan 16 22:02:36 2005	36993754		SellMarket	USD/JPY	300	102.08	299.9119	500.08
Mon Jan 17 01:16:34 2005	37000095	36993754	ClosePositionS	USD/JPY	300	102.14	299.9119	499.90
Mon Jan 17 01:35:22 2005	37000379		SellMarket	EUR/USD	200	1.31130	262.2600	499.90
Mon Jan 17 03:11:50 2005	37013300		SellEntry	EUR/USD	300	1.31600	0.0000	499.90
Mon Jan 17 05:04:34 2005	37033432		BuyEntry	EUR/USD	100	1.30700	0.0000	499.90
Mon Jan 17 10:35:22 2005	37062036	37033432	CloseOrder	EUR/USD	100	1.30700	0.0000	499.90
Mon Jan 17 10:35:51 2005	37062054	37000379	BuyMarket	EUR/USD	100	1.30810	130.8100	500.22
Mon Jan 17 10:36:25 2005	37062120	37000379	ClosePositionS	EUR/USD	100	1.30820	130.8050	500.53
Mon Jan 17 10:36:40 2005	37062129	37013300	CloseOrder	EUR/USD	300	1.31600	0.0000	500.53
Mon Jan 17 16:00:00 2005	37086750		Interest	USD		1.31600	0.0273	500.56
Tue Jan 18 04:34:34 2005	37156691		BuyMarket	GBP/USD	100	1.86260	186.2700	500.56
Tue Jan 18 04:35:13 2005	37156967	37156691	ChangeTrade	GBP/USD	100	1.86260	0.0000	500.56
Tue Jan 18 04:37:47 2005	37158033	37156691	CloseTradeB	GBP/USD	100	1.86350	186.3800	500.65
Tue Jan 18 10:12:57 2005	37244403		BuyMarket	EUR/USD	100	1.30163	130.1530	500.65
Tue Jan 18 11:25:33 2005	37250815	37244403	ClosePositionB	EUR/USD	100	1.30290	130.3150	500.78
Tue Jan 18 16:00:00 2005	37291047		Interest	USD		1.30290	0.0274	500.80

TABLE 1.6   Trade History
Source: Oanda.

Generally, here are 10 questions the trader can answer by trading the demo first:

1. How active are the dealer's quotes? Do they update smoothly or do they sit listlessly, only to jump 3 to 5 points at a time?
2. How wide is the spread between bid and ask?
3. Does the spread widen or it is fixed?
4. What kind of charting and news capabilities does the platform offer? Are they built in or added on?
5. Does the platform provide back-testing capabilities?
6. Can the platform run automated trading strategies?
7. Does the platform accept wireless trading? How stable is it? What fail-safe measures are there to make sure that orders actually went through? Is the dealing desk accessible by phone or through computer only?
8. What are the interest policies of the dealer?
9. What does reporting look like?
10. Does the platform require a separate software download or can it be traded through any browser via a Java applet?

In the end demo trading not only is important at the start of a trader's foray into forex but it also is a vital tool even after he begins to trade live. Expert traders, just like expert scientists, continue to probe and explore their craft even after having mastered it. Just as accomplished scientists continue to challenge themselves with unconventional experiments, so do seasoned traders pursue and refine new ideas on the demo accounts even as they trade their established setups live. In trading, one truth is incontrovertible: While there is no guarantee that your success in demo trading will translate into profits in a real account, a strategy that does not make money in the demo almost assuredly would be a failure in real life as well. One of the best aspects of forex is that laboratories are free—why not use them?

CHAPTER 2

Is It All Just Random?

According to many academics, technical analysis is a pure waste of time. Price, they claim, is absolutely random. Using patterns and indicators to predict its behavior is no different and no less primitive than reading entrails of a dead animal in order to divine your future. One of the favorite tricks of the pure randomness crowd is to have the random function in Microsoft Excel generate a series of numbers and then plot it on a graph. Admittedly, when many technically oriented traders are confronted with a seemingly nice chart pattern only to be told later that it's all random, they experience a loss of confidence. Is it all a ruse? Is technical analysis useless? Are we hopelessly wasting our time trying to learn its precepts? No, no, and no.

Price patterns are no more random than all human behavior—that is to say, they can be quite accurately predicted in general but quite often miss in the specific. Let's play the following game. Your job is to observe a wealthy Upper East Side businessman (for fun we'll assume that he always wears a dark blue pin-striped suit and yellow polka-dotted tie and is known to all as Mr. X) as he leaves his Park Avenue penthouse to walk 20 blocks to his high-rise office in the famous Met Life Insurance building. If you can accurately predict when he will appear in the door of his apartment building you win $1,000. If you are wrong you lose $1,000. What do you think your chances of winning would be if you simply had to choose morning or afternoon? How about if you were required to call the time to the hour? What about to the minute? The second? The millisecond? Of course, the more precise you had to be the less likely you would be right and the more likely you would lose money. File that thought away, because we will come back to this very important concept later in the book. In the meantime, answer this question: Are the activities of Mr. X random just because you cannot consistently predict his appearance at the door of his apartment building to the second or the millisecond of occurring? Of course not.

In fact Mr. X's behavior is highly predictable. If you observe him long enough you might know that on Fridays he seldom ventures out, preferring to work at home. Or that during Christmas week he doesn't go to the office at all, leaving the city altogether. Or perhaps that on particularly pleasant mornings he likes to linger on his balcony and smell the flowers planted in his flower boxes before heading off to the office. You would obtain all this information through observation—which is what speculation really is. The more you observed the better your information would become. Yet would you ever be able to bet your life savings on any one outcome of Mr. X's behavior? No, not if you were smart—because all of Mr. X's actions, like all human behavior and like all life, has an element of chaos to them. One Christmas week, for example, he may have been involved in a multibillion-dollar deal and therefore gone to his office every day. Another time he may have been bedridden with the flu and not have come out for days. Yet another day a neighbor's dog might have unexpectedly jumped on him in the elevator and torn his pants, necessitating a trip back upstairs and delaying his appearance at the door by more than 15 minutes.

To an untrained novice unaccustomed to Mr. X's habits, these changes of behavior would connote randomness and the player will most likely give up on the game after losing several thousand dollars, arguing that Mr. X's actions are completely unpredictable. But a skilled observer would understand that these deviations are simply the result of the normal degree of chaos in Mr. X's life. An expert in Mr. X's movements would know with a high degree of certainty that on most mornings Mr. X would appear at the door of his apartment building before 8 A.M., and the expert would be able to collect $1,000 making that bet.

Price data exhibits very similar dynamics. Unlike ivory-towered academicians, veteran traders who actually observe price action day in and day out for thousands of days at a time, realize that what is most striking about price behavior is not its wild randomness, but rather its mundane repetitiveness. Price patterns repeat themselves over and over and over again on many different time scales. What is different each time—and what makes trading sometimes maddeningly frustrating—is the amplitude of the move. Sometimes breakouts can last for 100 points and sometimes only for 10—just as sometimes Mr. X will have 100 uninterrupted days of punctually walking to his office and sometimes his schedule will be wildly skewed as other events in his life cause a temporary change of pattern.

Observation through technical analysis simply provides the trader a degree of expectancy but absolutely no guarantee that any particular trade analysis will be correct. Nevertheless, the greater the degree of expectancy, the better the trader's edge and the stronger the chance of ultimate success. After all, markets are not some robotic mechanisms that can be studied with keen dispassion through some elegant mathematical models. They are living, breathing organisms made up of millions of traders.

What do we trade in FX? I often ask this question at seminars. I get many answers but rarely the right one, for what we trade in FX is what is traded in all markets—sentiment. Fundamental factors shape and manufacture sentiment, while technical analysis expresses it. Price patterns are simply the reflection of repetitive human reactions of fear and greed to ever-changing news flow. They are not some randomly generated numbers from an Excel spreadsheet, even though they may look very similar. This is the critical flaw of pure randomness theorists—just because random functions can often mimic price patterns does not mean that price patterns themselves are random.

CHAPTER 3

The Secret to Trading

Here is the secret to all trading.

Ready?

Prices will either trend or range. That's all there is to it. It really is that simple but clearly not that easy. These two discrete properties of price require diametrically opposite mind-sets and money management techniques. Knowing when to apply each is what makes trading so difficult. Fortunately, the FX market is uniquely suited to accommodate both styles, providing either trend or range traders with opportunities for profit. Since trend seems to be the more popular subject, let's examine it first.

What is trend? The simplest definition of trend is higher lows in an uptrend and lower highs in a downtrend. Some traders define trend as prices remaining within an upward or downward sloping 20-period moving average. Yet others may draw trend lines or channels. I have my own definition, involving Bollinger bands, which I will discuss later in the book, but regardless of how one defines trend, the goal of trend trading is the same—join the move early and hold the position until the trend exhausts itself. The basic mind-set of the trend trader is "I am right or I am out," and his governing philosophy boils down to this: Do today what happened yesterday. The implied bet all trend traders make is that price will continue to follow its current direction. If it doesn't, there is little reason to hold on to the trade. Therefore, trend traders typically place very tight stops and often make several forays into the market in order to establish a proper entry.

By nature, trend trading generates far more losing trades than winning trades and requires rigorous risk control in order to achieve profits. The usual rule of thumb is that trend traders should never risk more than 1.5 to 2.5 percent of their capital on any given trade. On a $10,000 account trading 100,000-unit standard lots, that means stops as small as 15 to 25 pips behind the entry price. Clearly, in order to practice such a method, a trader must be confident that the market being traded is highly liquid. Of course the currency market is not only the most liquid market in the world but also the most fluid. Since the market trades 24 hours per day 5 days a week, it eliminates much of the gap risk found in exchange-based markets. Certainly gaps occur in FX, but not nearly as frequently as they happen in stock or bond markets, so slippage is far less of a problem.

When trend traders are right about the trade the profits can be enormous. This dynamic is especially true in FX where high leverage greatly magnifies the gains. It's not unusual to see a currency trend trader double his money in a short period of time if he catches a strong move. Here is a possible scenario of how it can be done. A trader starts out with $10,000 in his account. He uses a strict rule of 20-pip stops to limit his losses to 2 percent of capital. He may get stopped out five, six, or even ten times in a row, but if he finally catches a large move such as the 1,600-point decline in EUR/USD from January to July of 2005, his one-lot purchase would generate $16,000 in profit, easily increasing his account by 200 percent in a matter of months.

Of course few traders have the discipline to take constant stop-losses. Most traders dejected by a series of bad trades tend to become stubborn and fight the market, often placing no stops at all or removing the ones already in place. This is the time when FX leverage can become most dangerous. The same process that quickly produces profits can also generate massive losses. The end result is that many undisciplined traders suffer margin calls and lose most of their speculative capital on one or two bad trades.

Trading trend with discipline can be extremely difficult because if the trader uses high leverage he leaves little room to be wrong. Trading with very tight stops can result in 10 or even 20 consecutive stop-outs before a trader can find a trade with enough momentum and directionality to succeed.

For this reason many traders prefer to trade range-bound strategies. The typical process of range-bound trading involves isolating currencies that are trading in price channels and then selling at the top of the channel and buying at the bottom of the channel. This can be a very lucrative strategy, but in its essence it is still a trend-based idea, albeit one that anticipates an imminent countertrend. (What is a countertrend, after all, except a trend going the other way?)

True range traders don't care about direction. The underlying assumption of range traders is that no matter which way the currency is traveling at present it will most likely return to its point of origin. Range traders adhere to the concept of reversion to the mean. In fact, range traders bet on the possibility that prices will trade through the same levels over and over again, and their goal is to harvest all those oscillations for profit.

Clearly, range trading requires a completely different money management technique. Instead of looking for just the "right" entry, range traders actually prefer to be wrong at the outset, so they can build a trading position. For example, imagine that EUR/USD is in an uptrend and currently trading at 1.3000 (see Figure 3.1). A range trader may decide to short the pair at that level and every 100 pips higher, and then buy a portion of the trade back as it retraces every 100 pips down. His assumption is that eventually the pair will return to that original 1.3000 level. If EUR/USD indeed rises to 1.3500 and then turns back down to 1.3000, then the range trader will have been able to garner a handsome profit, especially if the currency moves back and forth in its climb to 1.3500 and its fall to 1.3000.

However, as we can see from this example, a range-bound trader will need to have very deep pockets in order to implement this strategy. In range trading, employing large leverage can be devastating, as positions can often go against the trader for many points in a row and, if he is not careful, trigger a margin call before the currency eventually turns.

Fortunately, the FX market provides a flexible solution for this type of trading. Most retail FX dealers offer mini lots of 10,000 units rather than

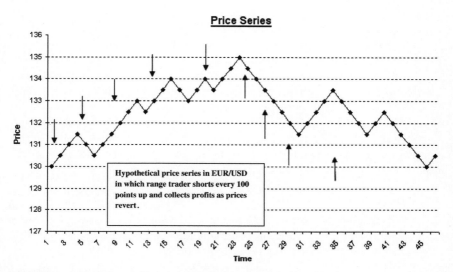

FIGURE 3.1 Hypothetical Range Trading Example

100,000 lots. For a pair like EUR/USD, in a 10,000-unit lot each individual pip is worth only $1 instead of $10 so the same hypothetical trader with a $10,000 account risking 2 percent per trade can have a stop-loss budget of 200 pips instead of only 20 pips. Even better, many dealers allow customers to trade in units of 1,000 or even 100-unit increments. Under that scenario our range trader trading 1,000-unit positions could withstand a 2,000-pip drawdown (with each pip now worth only 10 cents) before triggering a stop-loss. This flexibility allows range traders plenty of room to run their strategies.

Because FX dealers do not charge commissions and will quote the same price regardless of whether a customer wants to deal for 100 units or 100,000 units, a range-trading strategy can be implemented with even a small account of $1,000, as long as the trader properly sizes his trades. Granted, this method is the trading equivalent of collecting pennies and nickels, but it is the only proper way to implement a range strategy without assuming a large risk of blowout.

TRENDING CURRENCIES

Which currencies tend to trend more? That is, of course, an impossible question. The obvious answer is that at any given time any pair can find itself in a trend or range environment. Still, as general rule of thumb, the majors and the commodity pairs tend to trend more since they directly express the big macroeconomic events of the day while the crosses (currency pairs that do not have USD in them) tend to be more range-bound.

For a technically oriented trader, one of the great aspects of this market is that unlike the stock market, which contains thousands of equities, the FX market trades only four major pairs and three commodity pairs of currencies. Certainly, there are many more currencies in the world than that, but these minor currencies, known as exotics, are not traded by many retail dealers and often have extraordinarily wide bid/ask spreads because of lack of liquidity. The vast majority of speculative capital in the currency market is concentrated in the following major pairs, and all retail FX dealers will make tight markets in these instruments.

The Majors
- EUR/USD   Euro–U.S. dollar
- USD/JPY   U.S. dollar–Japanese yen
- GBP/USD   British pound–U.S. dollar
- USD/CHF   U.S. dollar–Swiss franc

It is certainly understandable why the United States, the European Union, and Japan would have the most active and liquid currencies in the world, but why the United Kingdom? After all, India has a larger gross domestic product (GDP) ($3.3 trillion vs. $1.7 trillion for the UK), while Russia's GDP ($1.4 trillion) and Brazil's GDP ($1.5 trillion) almost match the United Kingdom's total economic production. The explanation, as with so much of the FX market, is simply tradition. The United Kingdom was the first economy in the world to develop sophisticated capital markets, and at one time it was the British pound, not the U.S. dollar, that served as the world's reserve currency. Because of this legacy and because of London's primacy as the center of FX dealing in the world, the pound is considered one of the major currencies of the world. However, because the United Kingdom's economy is approximately one-tenth the size of those of the United States or European Union, liquidity in the pound can be a problem. That's why the GBP/USD will often move several hundred points per day as traders scramble to either cover or establish positions. For this reason the pound tends to be streakiest of the major pairs, which can be wonderful if you are on the right side of the trend and unbelievably painful if you are not.

The Swiss franc takes its place among the four majors because of Switzerland's famed neutrality, fiscal prudence, and long history of safety. At one time 40 percent of the "Swissie" was physically backed by gold, and to many traders in the FX market it is still known as "liquid gold." In times of geopolitical turmoil or economic recessions, traders flock to the Swiss franc as a liquid safe haven for assets.

The largest major pair—in fact, the most liquid financial instrument in the world—is the EUR/USD. This pair turns over almost $1 trillion per day in volume as trading proceeds from Tokyo to London to New York. The two currencies represent the two largest economic entities in the world—the United States with an annual GDP of $11 trillion and the euro zone with GDP of approximately $10.5 trillion. Although in recent years U.S. economic growth has been far better than the euro zone's, the euro-zone economy generates net trade surpluses while the United States runs chronic trade deficits. The superior balance sheet position of the euro zone and the sheer size of the euro-zone economy have made the euro an attractive alternative reserve currency to the dollar. Many central banks of the world, including those of China, Russia, Brazil, and South Korea, have diversified some of their reserves into the euro. Clearly this process takes time and it highlights one of the key attributes of successful trend trading—the need for a much longer-term outlook. Take a look at Figures 3.2 and 3.3, two charts using a three simple moving average (3 SMA) filter.

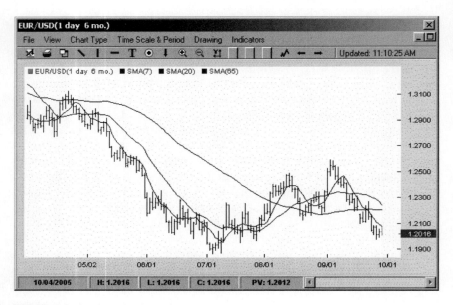

FIGURE 3.2 EUR/USD Daily Perspective
Source: FXtrek IntelliChart™. Copyright 2001–2005 FXtrek.com, Inc.

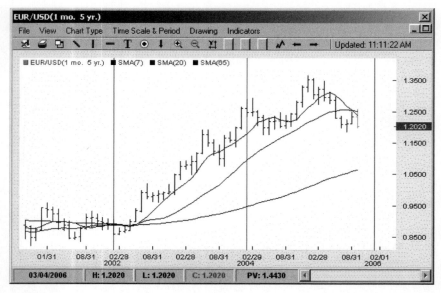

FIGURE 3.3 EUR/USD Monthly Perspective
Source: FXtrek IntelliChart™. Copyright 2001–2005 FXtrek.com, Inc.

The 3 SMA filter is a good way to gauge the strength of trend. The basic premise of this filter is that if the short-term trend (7 SMA), the intermediate-term trend (20 SMA), and the long-term trend (65 SMA) are all aligned in one direction, then the trend is strong. The importance of the 3 SMA filter does not lie in the specific SMA values, but rather in the interplay of the short-/intermediate-/long-term price trends as demonstrated by the three simple moving averages. As long as you use reasonable proxies for the short-, intermediate-, and long-term trends, the 3 SMA filter will provide valuable analysis.

Looking at the EUR/USD from two time perspectives, we can see how different the trend signals can be. Figure 3.2 displays the daily price action for the summer months of 2005, which shows choppy movement with a clear bearish bias. Figure 3.3, however, uses the monthly data for the past five years and paints a very different picture. According to Figure 3.3, EUR/USD has been in a clear up trend despite some very sharp corrections along the way.

Warren Buffett, the famous investor who is well known for making long-term trend trades, has been heavily criticized for holding on to his massive long EUR/USD position, which has recently suffered some losses. Looking at Figure 3.3, which offers a much longer time perspective, it becomes much clearer why Mr. Buffett often has the last laugh in the financial markets.

The Commodity Currencies

- USD/CAD   U.S. dollar–Canadian dollar
- AUD/USD   Australian dollar–U.S. dollar
- NZD/USD   New Zealand dollar–U.S. dollar

The three most liquid commodity currencies in FX markets are USD/CAD, AUD/USD, and NZD/USD. The Canadian dollar is affectionately known as the "loonie," the Australian dollar as the "Aussie," and the New Zealand dollar as the "kiwi." These three nations are tremendous exporters of commodities and often trend very strongly in concert with demand for their primary export product. Figure 3.4 shows the performance of the Canadian dollar and crude oil prices. Canada is the largest exporter of oil to the United States, with almost 10 percent of its GDP comprised of the energy exploration sector. Because USD/CAD trades inversely (it falls as CAD goes up in value), Canadian dollar strength creates a downtrend in the pair.

Although Australia does not have many oil reserves, the country is a very rich source of precious metals and iron ore and is also the second-largest exporter of gold in the world. In Figure 3.5 note how a rally in gold from December 2002 to November 2004 coincided with a very strong up move in the Australian dollar.

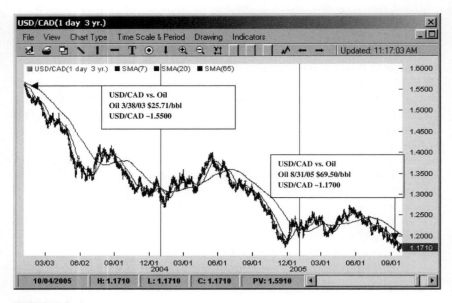

FIGURE 3.4 USD/CAD versus Oil
Source: FXtrek IntelliChart™. Copyright 2001–2005 FXtrek.com, Inc.

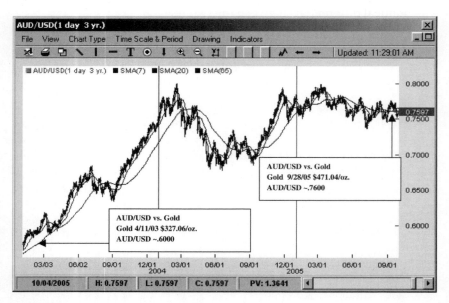

FIGURE 3.5 AUD/USD versus Gold
Source: FXtrek IntelliChart™. Copyright 2001–2005 FXtrek.com, Inc.

CROSSES ARE TYPICALLY BEST FOR RANGE TRADING

In contrast to the majors and commodity block currencies, which can offer traders some of the strongest and longest trending opportunities, currency crosses often present the best range-bound trades. Crosses are simply combinations of majors and commodity currencies that do not have the U.S. dollar as part of the pairing. There are more than 18 combinations of major and commodity crosses, but some of the most actively traded include the following pairs:

- *EUR/JPY*—one of the most active pairings in the currency world, as it is the primary hedging instrument for the massive amount of trade between Europe and Asia.
- *GBP/JPY*—a very active cross among carry trade speculators because of the wide interest rate differentials that have developed between the UK and Japan since the beginning of the millennium.
- *AUD/JPY*—yet another widely traded carry-based cross that often attracts flows from Japanese pensioners seeking income from much higher-yielding Australian bonds.
- *EUR/GBP*—a very active cross that reflects trade flows and economic performance disparities between the UK and the euro zone.
- *EUR/CHF*—a more muted cross that often trades on economic and political differentials between the two regions.
- *CAD/JPY*—one of the purest ways to express an opinion on oil in the currency market, as Canada is the primary beneficiary of high oil prices in the industrialized world while Japan is the greatest victim.

The EUR/CHF is perhaps the best range-bound pair to trade at the present time. The key reason for such tight trading is that there is very little difference between the growth rates of Switzerland and the European Union. Both regions run current account surpluses and adhere to fiscally conservative policies. Furthermore, as Switzerland's largest trading partner and biggest export market, the euro zone and its economic fate greatly impact Switzerland's economy.

One strategy for range traders is to determine the parameters of the range for the pair, divide them by a median line, and simply buy below the median and sell above it. For example, in EUR/CHF, range traders could establish 1.5600 as the top and 1.5280 as the bottom of the range with 1.5440 as the median line demarcating the buy and sell zones (see Figure 3.6).

Range traders are agnostic about direction. They simply want to sell relatively overbought conditions and buy relatively oversold conditions. One of the reasons that cross currencies are so attractive for this strategy is because imbalances between culturally and economically similar countries

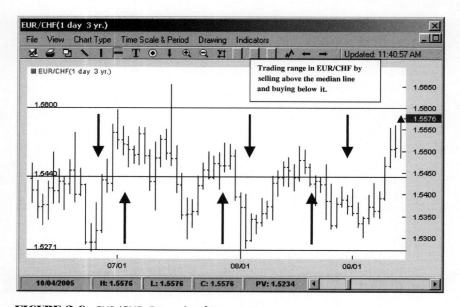

FIGURE 3.6 EUR/CHF: Example of Narrow Range
Source: FXtrek IntelliChart™. Copyright 2001–2005 FXtrek.com, Inc.

tend to return to equilibrium. The same cannot be said for stocks. It is hard to fathom that Switzerland would go into a depression while the rest of Europe merrily expands. In contrast, it is quite easy to imagine that while General Motors may file for bankruptcy Daimler Chrysler would continue to do business. Because currencies represent macroeconomics, they are not nearly as susceptible to microeconomic risk as individual company stocks and are therefore much safer to range trade.

Nevertheless, risk is present in all speculation, and traders should never range trade any pair without a stop. A reasonable strategy is to employ a stop at one-half the amplitude of the total range. In the case of EUR/CHF, the stops would be at 160 pips above the high and 160 below the low. In other words, if this pair reached 1.5800 or 1.4800 the trader should stop himself out of the trade because range would most likely have been broken.

INTEREST RATES—THE FINAL PIECE OF THE PUZZLE

While EUR/CHF can have a relatively tight 320-pip range, a pair like GBP/JPY has seen a far larger 3,000-pip range (see Figure 3.7). What is the difference? Interest rates.

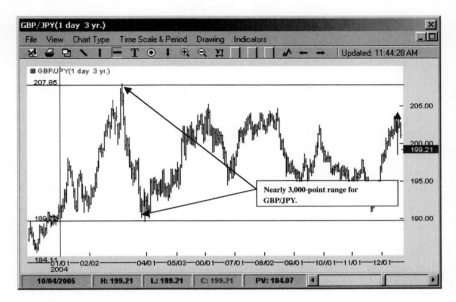

FIGURE 3.7 GBP/JPY: Example of Wide Range
Source: FXtrek IntelliChart™. Copyright 2001–2005 FXtrek.com, Inc.

At the time of writing in August 2005, Switzerland had an interest rate of 75 basis points and euro-zone rates were 200 basis points, creating a differential of only 125 basis points. The interest rates in the United Kingdom, however, stood at 475 basis points, while in Japan—which was still mired in deflation—rates remained at 0 basis points for a whopping 475-basis-point differential. The rule of thumb in FX is the larger the interest rate differential the more volatile the pair.

Table 3.1 lists various crosses, their interest rate differentials, and the maximum pip movement from high to low over the past 12 months.

TABLE 3.1 Range Values versus Interest Rate Differentials

Currency Pair	Central Bank Rates as of 10/01/2005 (Basis Points)	Interest Rate Spread (Basis Points)	12-Month Trading Range in Pips
AUD/JPY	AUD-550 JPY-0	550	1,400
GBP/JPY	GBP-450 JPY-0	450	2,100
GBP/CHF	GBP-450 CHF-75	350	1,500
USD/JPY	USD-375 JPY-0	425	1,900
EUR/JPY	EUR-200 JPY-0	225	1,300
EUR/CHF	EUR-200 CHF-75	125	350
CHF/JPY	CHF-75 JPY-0	100	800

While the relationship is far from perfect, it is certainly substantial. Note how pairs with wider interest rate spreads typically trade in larger ranges. Thus, when contemplating range-trading strategies in FX, traders must be keenly aware of rate differentials and adjust for volatility accordingly. Failure to take interest rate differentials into account could turn potentially profitable range-trading ideas into losing propositions. The FX market is incredibly flexible in its ability to accommodate both trend and range traders, but proper knowledge is key to successful implementation of either range-trading or trend-trading strategies.

CHAPTER 4

Show Me
the Data!

There are three basic ways to display price data in a chart. The simplest and perhaps least useful is via a line chart. The line chart displays one single point of price per unit of time and therefore offers only the most basic data to the trader. Figure 4.1 is an example of a line chart in the EUR/USD using the daily time frame. Notice how the chart offers only the most basic data regarding price action, hiding all of the intraday volatility. Because of this property, few technical traders ever use line charts as their source of analysis, yet perhaps more should. It is precisely because of their simplicity that line charts could be a valuable tool for quickly ascertaining trend or trend exhaustion. By eliminating most of the price action, line charts also in effect eliminate a lot visual noise, allowing the trader to focus on the core price movement.

Bar charts are the next way to display price, and they encompass far more information than simple line charts. Bar charts show the open, high, low, and close of the instrument for a particular time frame. Figure 4.2 depicts the basic visual parameters of the bar chart.

Bar charts undoubtedly contain more data than the simple line charts. Most importantly, they show the highs and lows for the given time period, providing the trader with a clear idea of the magnitude of volatility. Note, for example, the same price data displayed as a bar chart and greater depth of information that it conveys. Most importantly, the bar chart offers the trader clues to the power of the move. See how in Figure 4.3 a close near the top of the day's range hints at further upside momentum to come.

The final type of chart has become the most popular way to display

41

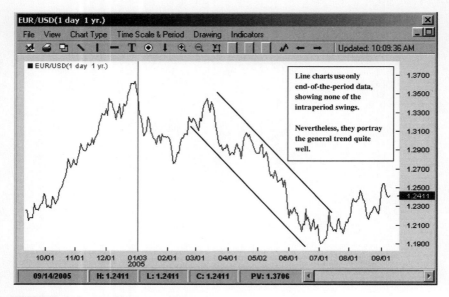

FIGURE 4.1 EUR/USD Line Chart
Source: FXtrek IntelliChart™. Copyright 2001–2005 FXtrek.com, Inc.

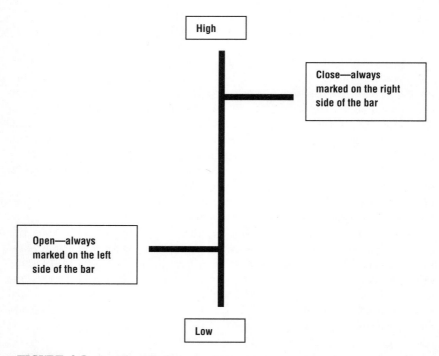

FIGURE 4.2 Bar Chart Basics

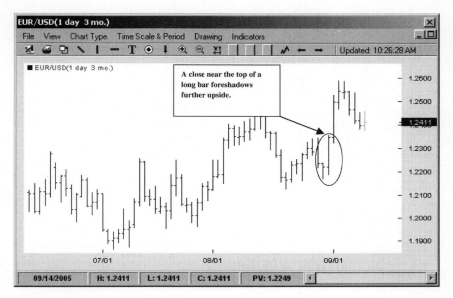

FIGURE 4.3 EUR/USD Bar Chart
Source: FXtrek IntelliChart™. Copyright 2001–2005 FXtrek.com, Inc.

price data today. Candlestick charts, first invented by rice traders in 17th-century Japan, come with their own lore. Legend has it that a 17th-century rice farmer used candlestick analysis to make 70 consecutive profitable trades. Because of candlesticks' exotic heritage and their incredible ability to produce descriptive images of price action in a highly compressed manner, candlestick adherents attribute near mystical powers when describing this tool's ability to predict price.

Candlesticks were first popularized in the West by Steve Nisson, who has written several authoritative books on the subject. For those truly interested in the subject matter, I suggest you refer to his work. For our purposes, however, only a basic understanding of candlesticks is necessary. Unlike many candlestick proponents, I find them almost useless for trading as a stand-alone instrument and valuable only when used in conjunction with other technical indicators. Nevertheless, like almost all other traders in FX, I use them exclusively on my charts for several reasons, not the least of which is the fact that they are far more aesthetically pleasing than line or bar charts and they do provide a very powerful visual shorthand for price action.

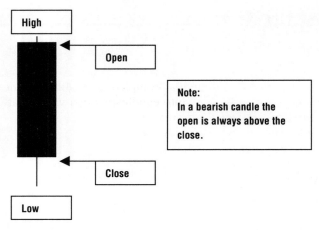

FIGURE 4.4   Bearish Candle

How is a candlestick constructed? The basic parameters of the candlestick include a body circumscribed by the open and the close and two wicks or shadows that demarcate the high and the low. If the close is lower than the open, then the candle is dark or bearish (see Figure 4.4). If the open is higher than the close, then the candle is white or bullish (see Figure 4.5).

There are numerous candlestick formations, but all of them essentially fall into three categories:

1. Breakout patterns
2. Indecision patterns
3. Reversal patterns

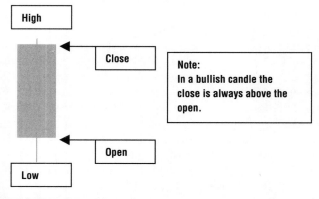

FIGURE 4.5   Bullish Candle

BREAKOUT PATTERNS

Bullish/Bearish Engulfing

The bullish engulfing pattern consists of two candlesticks; the first is black, and the second is a white candle that completely "engulfs" the first candle. The size and positioning of the white candlestick can vary greatly, but the critical feature of the pattern is that the second candle should be long and its body should completely encompass the wicks or shadows as well as the body of the smaller candle. The bigger the candle, the more bullish the signal. The bearish engulfing pattern works the exact same way except in reverse. Figures 4.6 and 4.7 show both bullish and bearish engulfing patterns.

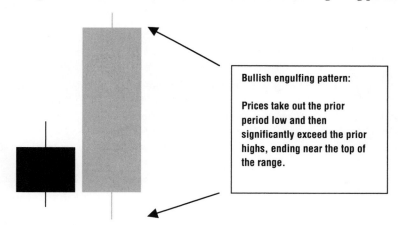

Bullish engulfing pattern:

Prices take out the prior period low and then significantly exceed the prior highs, ending near the top of the range.

FIGURE 4.6 Bullish Engulfing Pattern

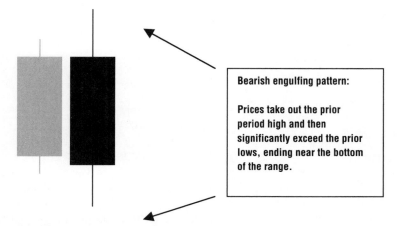

Bearish engulfing pattern:

Prices take out the prior period high and then significantly exceed the prior lows, ending near the bottom of the range.

FIGURE 4.7 Bearish Engulfing Pattern

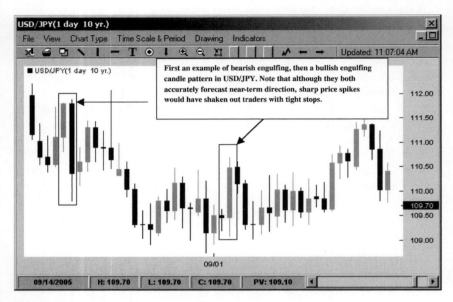

FIGURE 4.8 Bearish and Bullish Engulfing Patterns in USD/JPY
Source: FXtrek IntelliChart™. Copyright 2001–2005 FXtrek.com, Inc.

The bullish or bearish engulfing candlestick formation is considered by some to be a reversal pattern, but is in fact a very strong indication of a potential breakout or breakdown. Figure 4.8 shows both bullish and bearish engulfing formations, and as you can see the pattern occurs when bulls quickly sweep up all the outstanding offers or the bears hit every single bid. The underlying logic behind the pattern is that early smart money is positioning for a large directional move, and technically oriented traders would be wise to follow.

INDECISION PATTERNS

Doji Candle

A doji candle is characterized by a very small or almost nonexistent body and either long or short shadows. There are numerous varieties of dojis, with some examples found in Figures 4.9 through 4.13, but they all connote indecision on the part of the market. The basic dynamic of the doji is that buyers and sellers find themselves in an equilibrium as prices close at or near where they open after they explore the highs and lows of the range.

A simple doji candle, which displays a muted range and a close equal to the open.

FIGURE 4.9 Doji Candle

A long-legged doji candle, which shows a wide-ranging day with both bulls and bears at a standstill by the end of the period.

FIGURE 4.10 Long-Legged Doji

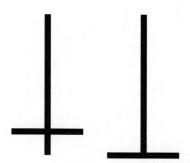

Two versions of the gravestone doji, which can often halt rallies dead in their tracks as it connotes that prices rose and then retraced all of their gains by returning to their open.

FIGURE 4.11 Gravestone Doji

The dragonfly doji is a rare formation, but when it happens it often presages a turnaround in prices as it shows that prices dipped but then recovered to opening levels.

FIGURE 4.12 Dragonfly Doji

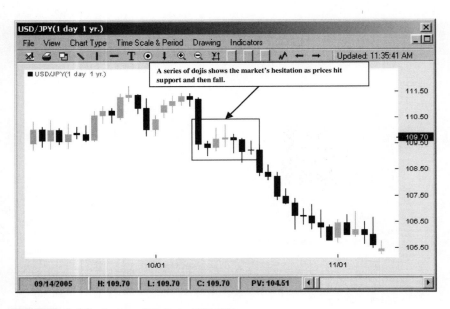

FIGURE 4.13 Series of Dojis in USD/JPY
Source: FXtrek IntelliChart™. Copyright 2001–2005 FXtrek.com, Inc.

Dark Cloud Cover

Yet another indecision pattern is the Dark Cloud Cover (see Figure 4.14). The Dark Cloud Cover is a two-candle pattern that occurs when a long white candle is followed by a black candle with an open above the previous candle's high but a close within the white candle's body and below its midpoint. Dark Cloud Cover is somewhat similar to a bearish engulfing, and many traders consider the pattern to be more of a reverse rather than a hesitation or indecision pattern; but in fact the Dark Cloud Cover by itself is not strong enough to be considered a reversal pattern. Traders should wait to see price action confirm the reversal before assuming that prices will change direction. Figure 4.15 shows the Dark Cloud Cover pattern in GBP/USD.

The key dynamic in price action behind the Dark Cloud Cover is that bulls, having taken prices to a new high, are unable to sustain their momentum and prices fall below the midpoint of the prior day's range. Though some interpret this price action as a serious sign of weakness, I think a more fair explanation is a pause in momentum. Therefore this pattern should be viewed as one of market indecision rather than necessarily a precursor to a price turn.

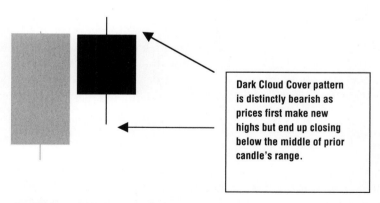

Dark Cloud Cover pattern is distinctly bearish as prices first make new highs but end up closing below the middle of prior candle's range.

FIGURE 4.14 Dark Cloud Cover Pattern

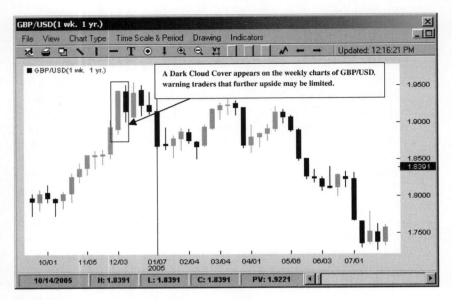

FIGURE 4.15 Dark Cloud Cover in GBP/USD
Source: FXtrek IntelliChart™. Copyright 2001–2005 FXtrek.com, Inc.

REVERSAL PATTERNS

For candlestick aficionados, the candlestick's ability to presage market turns and quickly identify trend exhaustion is this tool's greatest asset. There are numerous reversal patterns in candlestick theory, but for our purposes we will focus on the most common and popular formations.

The Harami

The Harami candlestick (*harami* in Japanese means "pregnant") is a two-candle formation that can flash either bullish or bearish signals depending on the sequence of candles. In Figure 4.16 we see a bearish Harami reversal where a large white candle is followed by a small dark one. For those of you more familiar with technical analysis, the Harami is a classic example of an "inside" day where the price action of today is completely inside the price range of the prior day. To Japanese traders, the formation looked like a baby (the small black candle) that came from the belly of the mother (the large white candle)—thus the name "pregnant." Regardless of the nomenclature, candlestick theory views the Harami as a reversal signal. The formation suggests that after a large up move that closes on the

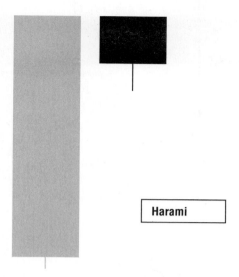

FIGURE 4.16 Harami Pattern

highs of the day bears are able to wrest control from the bulls, first by
stymieing further momentum and then by driving prices to close below
the day's open.

The Harami by itself is a relatively weak reversal signal as it could just
as easily suggest consolidation rather than a trend change. Nevertheless,
under certain circumstances, such as the example in Figure 4.17, it can
lead to a trend change.

Hammer or Hanging Man

The shooting star/reverse hammer and the hammer/hanging man candlestick formations (see Figures 4.18 and 4.19) are the opposite sides of the
same coin, but taken together they represent some of the strongest reversal signals among candlestick patterns. In the shooting star or reverse
hammer candlestick, prices explore the upper end of the range and are
quickly rejected. The end result is that prices not only fail to hold the
highs but actually end lower than where they opened. In the hammer or
hanging man candlestick the exact opposite dynamic occurs as prices test
the lows and are instantly bid up by bargain-hunting bulls. Both the shooting star and the hammer are most effective if they appear after a large directional price move. These patterns provide a very powerful visual
shorthand for trend exhaustion. Essentially what they are communicating
is that prices have reached a relative apex or nadir and these price levels

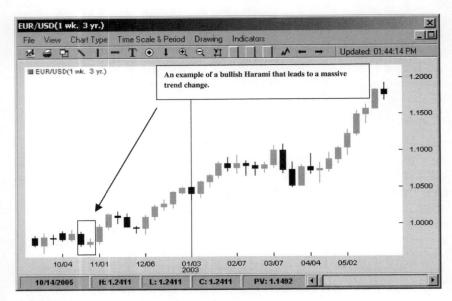

FIGURE 4.17 Bullish Harami in EUR/USD
Source: FXtrek IntelliChart™. Copyright 2001–2005 FXtrek.com, Inc.

FIGURE 4.18 Shooting Star or Reverse Hammer

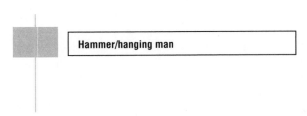

FIGURE 4.19 Hammer or Hanging Man

have been deemed by the marketplace to be either too expensive or too cheap. Some experts believe that the longer the wick or shadow in these patterns, the higher the probability that they have signaled a swing bottom or top. Figure 4.20 demonstrates both the shooting star and the hammer in action.

Morning Star/Evening Star

Morning star and evening star are simply more complex variations on the shooting star/hammer formations. In the morning star a long black candle is followed by a hammer, which in turn is followed by a long white candle (see Figure 4.21). The sequence is simply reversed and has a shooting star in the evening star formation (see Figure 4.22). What both of these candlestick patterns communicate, however, is the notion that control of the price action is slowly changing from sellers to buyers in the morning star pattern and from buyers to sellers in the evening star pattern. Some candlestick analysts will argue that the deeper the third candle penetrates into the first candle's price range, the greater the likelihood that prices will reverse. In effect, in both the evening and morning star formations the

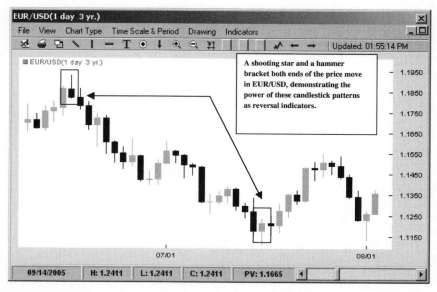

FIGURE 4.20 Reversals in EUR/USD with Shooting Star and Hammer
Source: FXtrek IntelliChart™. Copyright 2001–2005 FXtrek.com, Inc.

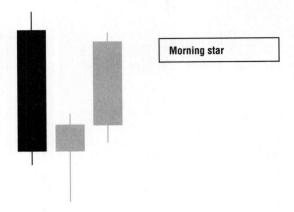

FIGURE 4.21   Morning Star

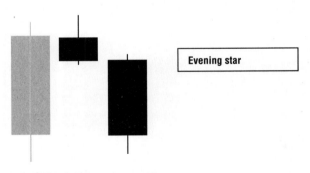

FIGURE 4.22   Evening Star

third candle is confirming the signals sent by the shooting star and the hammer and thus provides traders with more confidence to establish a position (see Figure 4.23).

Three Black Crows and Three Advancing White Soldiers

These two candlestick formations are considered to be the rarest and therefore the most powerful reversal patterns (see Figures 4.24 and 4.25). Even the names have tremendous resonance, with "Three Black Crows" sounding highly ominous and suggestive of carcasses and

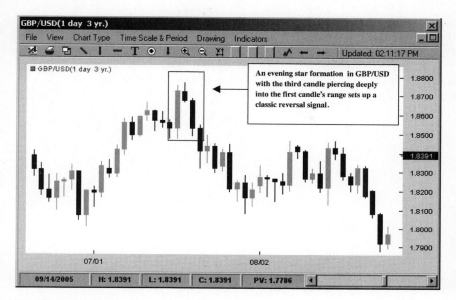

FIGURE 4.23   Evening Star in GBP/USD
Source: FXtrek IntelliChart™. Copyright 2001–2005 FXtrek.com, Inc.

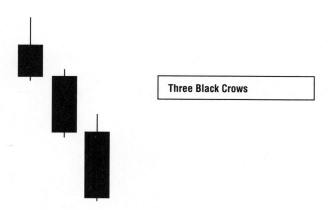

Three Black Crows

FIGURE 4.24   Three Black Crows

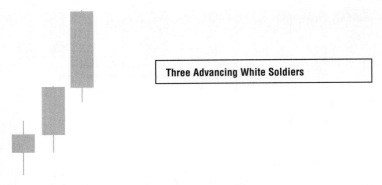

FIGURE 4.25 Three Advancing White Soldiers

death, while the name "Three Advancing White Soldiers" exudes confidence and strength.

In the Three Black Crows pattern, the signal is most powerful if the first black candle in the formation closes below the preceding white candle's body. This is the first clue to a trend reversal where today's high is lower than yesterday's high and today's low is below yesterday's low. Two more long-bodied consecutive down days then ensue. On each of these days, it appears as if the price wants to retest former highs by opening higher than the previous day's close, but by the end of each session the sellers regain control and prices drop to a new closing low (see Figure 4.26).

In the Three Advancing White Soldiers, the price dynamic is simply flipped over as the virtuous cycle takes over and prices continuously make new highs with the bulls wrestling control from the bears.

FINAL WORD ON CANDLESTICKS

There is no doubt that candlesticks have become the preferred way for technically oriented traders to display chart data. One need only look at any trader's desktop computer to find that an overwhelming majority look at price data through candlesticks even if most are not familiar with many of the arcane formations. As I noted, the purpose of this chapter is not to provide a comprehensive accounting of every pattern. Many authors far more talented and erudite that yours truly have already

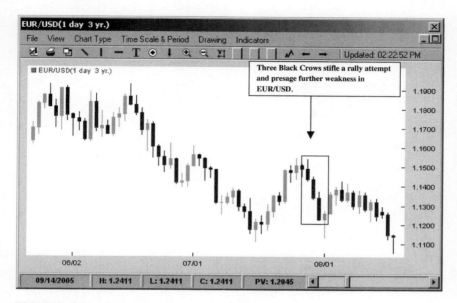

FIGURE 4.26 Three Black Crows in EUR/USD
Source: FXtrek IntelliChart™. Copyright 2001–2005 FXtrek.com, Inc.

done that. Rather, the idea here is to highlight the most important formations for day-to-day trading and to provide the basic understanding behind candlestick theory. Indeed, it is easy to see why candlesticks have become so popular. Their ability to visually compress and summarize the key events in the battle between the bulls and the bears for any given time frame is truly astounding. Nevertheless, as I noted before, taken by themselves candlestick signals are almost useless and will fool traders into many false trades if they choose to utilize them exclusively. Only when the candlestick patterns are placed into the broader context of overall price action as well as the supporting information from various indicators (which we discuss later on) do they provide high-probability actionable setups.

I hope that one point that this chapter has made is just how subjective some candlestick analysis is. Proper candlestick trading is far more a matter of art rather than science. It requires much screen time for traders to become familiar with and quickly recognize key patterns, which in real life are never quite as precise as they appear in the book. If there is one shorthand lesson to take away from candlestick analysis it's this: *The wick is the trick*. By elegantly separating the price action of the open and close from the highs and the lows, candles offer the trader an instant view of the strength of the underlying trend. That is why doji candles with their long wicks suggesting hesitation and indecision are so closely followed by many technical traders, as they provide a quick glimpse of actual price dynamics.

CHAPTER 5

Trend Is Your Friend?

Everybody loves a trend. Almost every trading book repeats the dictum "the trend is your friend" ad nauseum. Furthermore, most traders are much more comfortable trading with the trend, rather than against it. In FX, where strong trends tend to develop often as major economic themes seize the market for sometimes months at a time, trend trading is the preferred strategy of choice.

What is a trend? The basic, most common definition is higher lows for an uptrend or lower highs for a downtrend, both of which form stutter-step patterns in the price action. Note that trend is defined by the price action of the *lows* in a uptrend and *highs* in a downtrend, something that may appear at first to be counterintuitive but actually makes sense upon further reflection. Although most traders would define an uptrend as a series of higher highs, in fact prices can sometimes pause instead of rising. What makes an uptrend an uptrend is the failure of prices to go *down*; bulls overpower the bears and step up to buy every decline, which they perceive as an opportunity to acquire tradable assets at discount prices. The ever-higher slope of higher lows is what forms the uptrend on the charts. The process and the price dynamics work the exact same way except in reverse in downtrends.

Of course, this is an idealized definition of trend because prices rarely create such perfect patterns. Even in the strongest uptrends and the most vicious downtrends, prices will temporarily break below higher lows or above lower highs. In real life, price action tends to correct, retrace, and generally follow a two steps forward, one step backward scenario that can shake traders out of their positions at the slightest indication of change of trend. To combat this problem, technical traders have designed an array of tools to help them first determine if trend exists and then create strategies to stay in the trend for as long as possible.

TREND LINES

Perhaps nothing is more controversial in technical analysis than trend lines. Ridiculed by some as useless subjective squiggles on a chart and hailed by others as indispensable tools, they are the simplest method for trend determination in technical analysis. The rules for drawing trend lines vary, and therein lies the first problem. The premise behind the trend line is that in a uptrend the trader should draw a single straight line connecting the lowest swing low to the highest swing low and do the reverse in the downtrend. The idea is that price will then respect these boundaries. One very serious problem with trend lines is to know exactly where to draw them. Do you use the closing price or the highs and lows of the period? Do you adjust the slope for isolated spikes, or do you ignore them? Do you change the trend line based on the scale of your chart?

Note how in Figure 5.1 trend lines can have divergent slopes leading to very different conclusions as to the status of price action.

Proponents of trend lines argue that their true value is in capturing the natural rhythms of buying and selling. A more sophisticated use of the trend line is to design trend line channels that connect the lows of price action on one side and the highs on the other (see Figure 5.2). The classic technical analysis strategy is then to purchase the instrument at or near the support trend line and then sell it at or near the resistance.

The net effect is then to buy cheap and sell dear and be able to do so several times over as price progresses through time. This can be a very profitable strategy as long as price remains in the trend channel, but what happens when it breaks through? First and foremost, careful speculators should define clearly what constitutes a break of the trend line. Does a piercing of the line signify a break or must the price close through a trend line to be considered valid? How far must price extend beyond the trend line before it can be considered a legitimate break? More importantly, is a trendline break for only one price period enough?

There are of course no absolute answers, but certain rules can be applied with relative assurance. Generally a simple intraperiod piercing of a trend line when prices extend beyond it in a rush of buying fury in the case of a downtrend break, but then quickly retreat to close within the parameters of the line, is the weakest signal and for all intents and purposes is considered "noise" by most technicians. Understand that many profes-

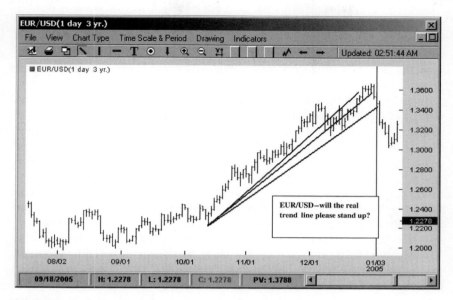

FIGURE 5.1 Different Possible Trend Lines in EUR/USD
Source: FXtrek IntelliChart™. Copyright 2001–2005 FXtrek.com, Inc.

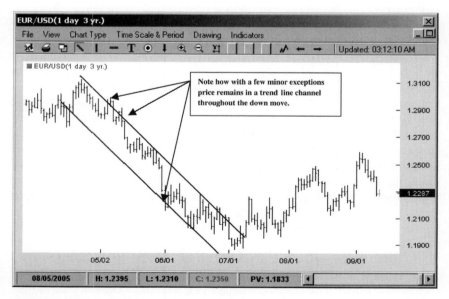

FIGURE 5.2 Trend Line Channel in EUR/USD
Source: FXtrek IntelliChart™. Copyright 2001–2005 FXtrek.com, Inc.

sional traders and dealers are well aware of these price channels, and they love nothing more than to run prices to those levels to pick off many stops clustered in that region. Because FX is the most leveraged market in the world, it is also one where most participants trade with hard stops. The failure to do so at such high leverage would quickly annihilate most trading accounts. Nevertheless, the flip side of this fact is that stop running is perhaps more prevalent in FX than in any other market. For this reason, intraperiod piercings of trend lines cannot really be considered valid breaks. A close above the trend line may carry more meaning, as it indicates that in the case of down trend line the buyers have found enough strength to overwhelm the sellers, who have typically been beating them up for days. Yet what meaning does the trend line break really hold? Does it predict change of trend? No, not at all. Certainly, sometimes a trend line break can mean that price action is ready to race the other way, but anyone who has traded for any period of time will attest that "V" bottoms and "Λ" tops are quite rare indeed. The best clue that can be gathered from trend line breaks is that the trend *may* be ending. What most frequently follows the end of a trend is not a strong countertrend but rather consolidation, which will tend to frustrate both bulls and bears alike as price action will generate many false breakouts and breakdowns while remaining essentially in the same place.

So what would provide the strongest evidence for a trend line break? First, price would have to close beyond, not just pierce, a particular trend line. In the case of a downtrend the close would have to be above the line. In the case of an uptrend the close would have to be below the line. Why such emphasis on the close? Because the basic premise of technical analysis is that the past matters, and the more recent, the more important its value. Technical analysis is the study of past price behavior to ascertain future direction. If prices are actually able to close above or below the key trend line, the assumption is that the consensus of the market may have materially changed. Like tectonic plates underneath the earth's surface, speculator sentiment may be shifting away from the present direction. Secondarily, if price over the next few periods is then able to stay above the trend line in case of a downtrend break, and vice versa for an uptrend break, then technicians would have stronger support for their thesis that the trend was changing. Finally, if prices return to the trend line but then bounce off, that would provide a final clue that a turn may have occurred (see Figure 5.3).

The fundamental principle of technical analysis is that once resistance is broken it becomes support, and once support is broken it becomes resistance. The common saying is that old support becomes new resistance and old resistance becomes new support. Why? The assumption behind this premise is that once traders have broken through a key

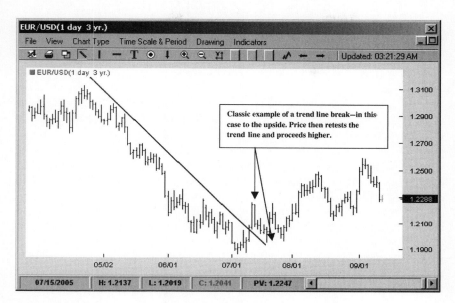

FIGURE 5.3 Trend Line Break in EUR/USD
Source: FXtrek IntelliChart™. Copyright 2001–2005 FXtrek.com, Inc.

level they will defend it vigorously. For example, in the case of an upside break the trading dynamic behind the move suggests that the bulls have decided that these particular prices represent true value for the currency pair as they overwhelm the bears and sweep away their stops. Now as price moves upward the bulls are validated in their thesis. However, the bears, though weakened, may decide to regroup at higher levels and try to push the price back down. As price declines back to the levels of the breakout the bulls may once again perceive value and decide to add to their positions. Furthermore, other players who have missed the original run-up will join the bidding as they now have an opportunity to position themselves for another run-up.

Does this work all the time? Of course not. New information can completely reconfigure the market's perception of value. That's why most successful technical traders also follow news. In surveys of various bank traders around the world, fundamental news is considered to be as critical to professional trading as technical analysis. Currencies, after all, are national assets, and they can be greatly affected by geopolitical events. To trade price action alone in a vacuum is to set yourself up for brutal shocks when news overwhelms technical patterns. However, in the absence of news prices do tend to respect the technical boundaries set by trend lines.

The reason is actually quite logical. When there is no news, the market is weighing the currently available information; therefore, prices that seemed like a bargain a few days ago may remain so today since no new information has hit the market.

William Gallacher in his famous antitechnical treatise *Winner Take All* (McGraw-Hill, 1993) noted that "trend lines cannot withstand serious critical scrutiny. It is born of geometric desire to suppose that bull and bear markets should proceed at a constant speed. It is ludicrous to try to confirm the constant speed of markets by trend lines." There is a lot of truth to that statement, as traders should be cautious not to attach too much significance to trend lines. As noted earlier, markets rarely move in elegant straight lines. However, during trends, price behaviors tend to assume a certain rhythm. In an uptrend, selling is constantly met with more buying and prices push ever higher as time moves forward. In a downtrend just the reverse occurs as every attempt to mark up prices is met with waves upon waves of selling as bids give way. Because the markets are a quintessential human activity, the dynamic is messy and often chaotic. Unlike machines that can spit out widgets with remarkable precision and complete detachment, human beings will overreact, panic, or become optimistic beyond all bounds. All of this behavior will be reflected in price action, which will faithfully record the madness of the crowd. For this reason alone I believe that trend lines should be best used as guidelines rather than some kind of inviolable vectors. Too often traders want the type of mathematical certainty with respect to trend lines that allows NASA scientists to point spacecraft on courses of thousands of miles away from earth and land them within inches of their destinations. That kind of attitude towards technical trading is only self-defeating. When it comes to trend lines, they should be called guidelines and used loosely to pinpoint the possible direction of price action. Ironically enough, trend lines may be of most value for traders who do not take them too seriously.

MOVING AVERAGES

A second method of identifying trend is the study of moving averages. Moving averages, unlike trend lines, provide far more definitive measures of support and resistance because they can be calculated mathematically with great precision. The most common form of moving average is the simple moving average (SMA), which is calculated by taking the sum of the closing price values of the tradable asset and dividing it by a specific number of periods. For a 10-period simple moving average the trader would add each individual price close and divide the total by 10. As each new period is added, the oldest period is dropped off and the average is recalculated. Simple moving averages are very much a lagging indicator, but they are very important to technical analysis nevertheless because they represent the consensus price of the market. By taking the average over a given period of time, traders can obtain an approximate idea of where the market believes the value lies. The most basic analysis states that if prices trade above a certain average they are in an uptrend and if they trade below they are in downtrend.

Aside from the simple moving average calculation, technicians have designed a variety of flavors of moving averages over the years. The next most common moving average is the exponential moving average (EMA), which differs from the simple moving average by weighting the most recent price data samples more heavily than the data from periods further back.

This process tends to make the EMA more responsive to recent price action and therefore eliminates some of the lag of the SMA. The idea behind the EMA is one common to much of technical analysis work—namely that the most recent price action is more valuable than prior price action. This idea sometimes works well, but it can also distort the overall tone of price action by underweighting events further past that may have an important effect on future market movement.

The exponential moving average is calculated as follows. Assuming the same 10-period time sample we used for our simple moving average, the exponential moving average would have each period multiplied by an exponent first before all the values are summed and divided by 10. One common formula is to have the EMA calculated by multiplying the most recent value by 10, the next most recent by 9, the one further back by 8, and so on, all divided by 10. You can clearly see that while the advantage of such a series is that it may respond faster to most recent price data, it does so at the expense of diminishing the value of the past data. While this type of calculation may provide the trader with faster response, it may also send out far more false signals.

I am of two minds about EMAs. On the one hand I can clearly see the value of weighting most recent price action to offer a trader faster clues to potential turns in price. On the other hand I feel that the function of stand-alone moving averages is to provide as accurate an approximation of price action as possible. By minimizing some parts of the sample while overemphasizing others, the price sample may become skewed and for this reason I prefer to use simple moving averages to get a true feel for direction. Ultimately the argument is really academic over the shorter time frames such as 20 days. Note how in

Figure 5.4 20-day SMA and 20-day EMA in the EUR/USD really do not deviate much from each other. On longer time frames the situation is quite different. Looking at the 200 SMA and 200 EMA in Figure 5.5, the divergence can be profound as the larger 200-period data sample with typically far greater variability in price will generate a far different reading in an SMA than in an EMA.

There are numerous technical systems centered on moving averages designed to help the technician to ascertain trend. The most basic and common way to utilize moving averages is to simply see if the current price is above or below a given moving average. Typically in an uptrend all price action is contained by the 20-period SMA. Why is this so? There is no exact answer and my observation simply comes from watching thousands upon thousands of chart patterns, but one logical explanation is that especially on a daily basis the number 20 represents a full month of trading and therefore serves as a good sample of market sentiment. Moving averages are notorious, though, for providing false signals when price action oscillates, so many traders create filters by designing moving average crossover systems. Typically these involve the use of a short-term moving average crossing a longer-term moving average to trigger a trade. If the

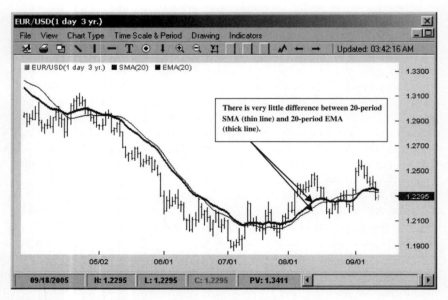

FIGURE 5.4 20 SMA versus 20 EMA
Source: FXtrek IntelliChart™. Copyright 2001–2005 FXtrek.com, Inc.

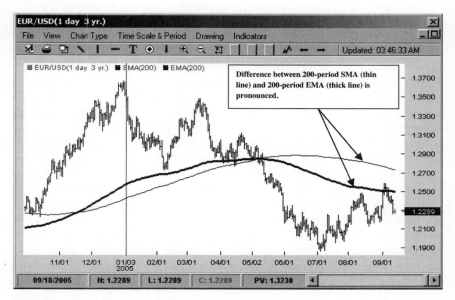

FIGURE 5.5 200 SMA versus 200 EMA
Source: FXtrek IntelliChart™. Copyright 2001–2005 FXtrek.com, Inc.

short-term average crosses the long-term average from the bottom, a buy signal is indicated. If it falls through the longer-term average from the top, this may signal further price weakness. The thinking behind these systems is that when the short-term average price has dipped below the long-term average price, the market is discounting the tradable asset as sellers mark down the price below long-term value. The converse is true when the short-term moving average moves above the long-term average. There are literally thousands of permutations of this setup, with traders utilizing every conceivable combination of averages to optimize their probability of success. Unfortunately, this methodology is just as vulnerable to choppy price action as the simple "price through the moving average" approach. Furthermore, the actual moving average crossover point often occurs at the worst possible price entry to the trader. The reason is optical deception that shows up on the charts versus the dynamic of what is happening in real time.

Rookie traders will often see a moving average crossover and perceive that the point of entry is at the intersection of the two moving averages. Seeing then how price action often follows in the direction of the cross they assume that this setup works well. In real life the actual moving average crossover occurs only after the price candle (i.e., the day's trading) has completed its period. If, say, in the case of a downtrend the price candle is particularly steep, the real-life entry for the trader is at the bottom of the candle rather than at the point of the cross. On the upside the exact same dynamic occurs in reverse. The end result is that the moving average crossover will often force the trader to sell the bottoms or buy the tops. This is the prototypical mistake of trend chasing rather than trend trading that frustrates so many traders using technical analysis techniques. Typically, after a severe move to the downside or a strong breakout to the upside, prices will pause and often retrace as short-term traders cover for profits while others fish for tops or bottoms. The net effect on the inexperienced trader who trades the moving average crossover blindly is to usually be in a losing trade from the moment of entry. While the trade ultimately may be correct, the disconcerting effect of instant losses will often force a panic stop out of the position with vows that all moving average crossover systems are useless (see Figure 5.6). Yet, as with all technical analysis concepts, it's the practitioner, not the tools, that determines success.

One interesting setup that uses moving averages is the triple moving average crossover. I like to use the 3-, 20-, and 65-period SMAs for my

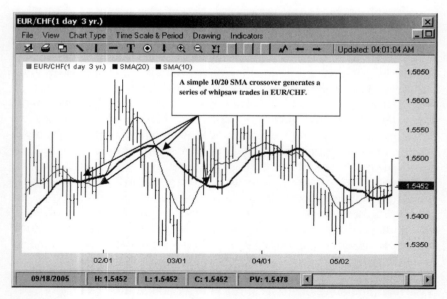

FIGURE 5.6 Whipsaw Trades with Moving Average Crossovers
Source: FXtrek IntelliChart™. Copyright 2001–2005 FXtrek.com, Inc.

setup, but the specific value of moving averages is immaterial. In fact, focusing on specific periodicity of moving averages is a useless task. There is very little difference between a 20-period and a 21-period or even 25-period moving average. Their variability is minuscule, and traders who spend their time trying to fine-tune just the right periodic average are engaging in nothing but retrofitting of data. The value of the 3 SMA filter is not in the particular time selection of averages, but in the fact that they are measuring the short-term, the intermediate-term, and the long-term directions of price. The idea behind this setup is that when the short-term average is above the intermediate-term average and the intermediate-term average is above the long-term average, prices are in an uptrend. When the positioning is reversed, with the intermediate-term below the long-term average and the short-term below the intermediate-term average, prices are in downtrend.

For the most part the value of the SMA setup is simply as an analysis tool. It can quickly and very effectively tell the trader if prices are in a trend, but it cannot tell the trader if that trend will continue. More importantly, the setup's primary value may be more as a negative filter rather than as a positive trigger. For example, a trend-oriented trader may choose to stand aside if there is any conflict among the three moving averages. If the intermediate-term average is above the long-term average but the short-term average has dipped below the intermediate-term average, the trend is unclear and the trend trader should look for a turn back up in price action before determining that the uptrend remains in place. This simple pause can save traders from untold mistakes by paring down trade selection to only the most consistent price patterns. Many traders often enter trades based on an outdated understanding of price action and then stubbornly hang on to losing positions, unwilling to accept the reality that price action has changed. For trend traders, the 3 SMA setup offers a simple yet logical analytic tool to test their assumptions. Unlike trend lines, which can be configured differently based on each trader's selection of price points, moving averages are completely objective in their readings (see Figure 5.7).

Although the 3 SMA filter is simply a trend detection tool and by itself cannot be used as an accurate trade trigger, there is one exception to the rule that is worth exploring. When price action compresses, the three moving averages will often begin to converge as the lack of volatility will make the average short-term, intermediate-term, and long-term price nearly identical. If at this point the three moving averages begin to fan out in proper alignment either up or down, as shown in Figure 5.8, then a trend trader should consider taking the price direction. The key reason that makes this particular variation of the setup so attractive is that the trade carries little risk. Since all of the moving averages are extremely

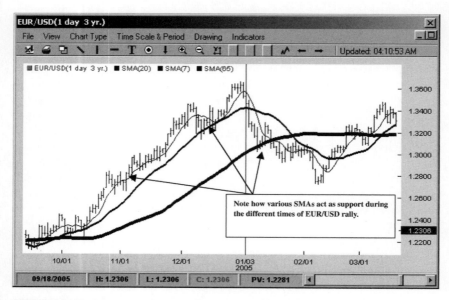

FIGURE 5.7 Support at Moving Averages in EUR/USD
Source: FXtrek IntelliChart™. Copyright 2001–2005 FXtrek.com, Inc.

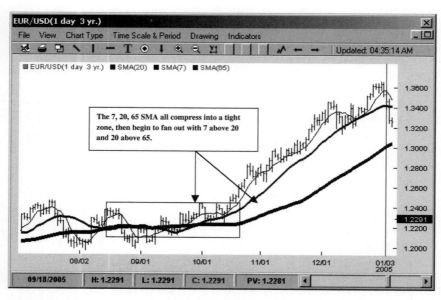

FIGURE 5.8 The Three Moving Average Filter
Source: FXtrek IntelliChart™. Copyright 2001–2005 FXtrek.com, Inc.

close to one another, it would not take a large adverse move in price to trigger a moving average crossover from the short-term average to the intermediate-term average and therefore indicate to the trader that the setup has failed. In actuality what this type of setup is showing is a classic volatility breakout. In times of market quiet when bulls and bears are in general agreement on price, volatility will contract, but as one camp assumes dominance price will begin to move in that direction. The 3 SMA filter is an easy visual representation of this dynamic, which when it occurs can lead to very powerful profits if the trend sustains itself for a long time.

AVERAGE DIRECTIONAL INDEX/DIRECTIONAL MOVEMENT INDEX

One very common technical trend detection indicator that I find absolutely worthless is the Average Directional Index (ADX)/Directional Movement Index (DMI). Invented by J. Welles Wilder, who was a tremendous innovator in the field of technical analysis, and some of whose indicators we will examine in detail later on, the ADX is comprised of three basic components: +DI, which indicates an up average of the tradable; –DI, which indicates the down average of the same instrument; and the ADX itself, which smooths the difference between the up prices and the down prices and then generates an oscillator reading between 0 and 100 that tells the trader whether the instrument is in a strong trend. The general rules are that readings above 20 indicate the presence of trend and readings below 20 suggest that markets are directionless. Like all of Wilder's work, the logic behind his analysis is sound. The idea is that as prices begin to find direction the difference between +DI and –DI will expand, providing the trader with valuable clues to price action. Unfortunately, in real life trading the ADX is a day late and dollar short affair. The indicator is woefully slow at producing any meaningful signals. Furthermore, since the ADX itself is directionally agnostic—simply telling the trader that a trend exists but unable to tell the direction of that trend—the trader can often be spectacularly faked out by relying on ADX readings alone. For example, prices may originally rise, causing ADX readings to increase, but then slowly change course and eventually begin a severe decline, while all the while ADX readings may be rising.

The ADX, of course, is simply communicating that price is in a trend—but not that it was in an uptrend, then has quickly changed direction, and is now declining. A trend still exists, and may even be increasing—but now it's a downtrend instead of an uptrend! It is easy to see how looking at ADX the trader can easily become confused by its signals. In-

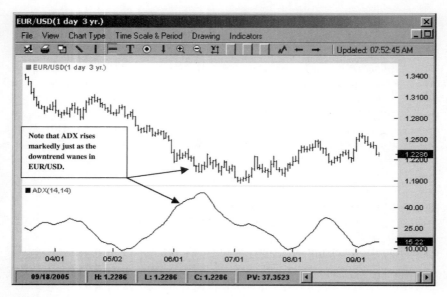

FIGURE 5.9 ADX versus Price Pattern
Source: FXtrek IntelliChart™. Copyright 2001–2005 FXtrek.com, Inc.

stead of being trend followers, traders using ADX become the ultimate trading sucker—they become trend chasers.

Although some traders actively use ADX for their trend trading work, and some even swear by its effectiveness, I find its usefulness limited at best. It is considered a classic trend indicator by technicians, which is why I have taken the time to discuss it, but I cannot leave without taking one final potshot at this tool. Note that when the price makes a sharp V move—that is, when prices suddenly reverse from declining to rising or vice versa—the ADX will often send completely contradictory messages to the trader. As the turn in price action is processed in its calculations, the ADX will indicate that the trend is actually weakening when in fact it's just beginning to find direction. Furthermore, just as prices may have reached a temporary peak or bottom, the ADX reading will rise, suggesting that a trend is now in place (see Figure 5.9)!

BOLLINGER BAND "BANDS"

Is there a more accurate way to glean trend? Yes, I believe there is. Surprisingly enough, one indicator that is often used for range-bound markets can be an extremely helpful tool for trend discovery. I discuss the Bollinger bands (BBs) in more detail in Chapter 10, but for now note that we will use them in a unique way to detect trends in the currency market.

Before we begin, let's first examine the underlying notion of trend. What is trend really? I will postulate that trend is actually a deviance in price. It is common wisdom in all markets that trends are generally rare. Typically, in all markets, including the currency market, prices stay in a range somewhere between 70 and 80 percent of the time. Therefore, when prices decide to trend they in fact deviate from the norm. What is one of the best tools to measure deviation in technical analysis? Bollinger bands, of course. The Bollinger band formula contains the standard deviation (SD) calculation within it. Bollinger bands measure the standard deviation of price away from its 20-period moving average. Here is where the use of Bollinger bands becomes quite interesting. If you superimpose a second set of Bollinger bands with a standard deviation setting of 1 onto the price chart that already has a set of BBs with a default setting of 2 standard deviations, you will instantly see that as prices begin to trend the majority of price action is captured within the 1 SD–2 SD Bollinger bands.

These Bollinger band "bands" divide the price action into three separate areas (see Figure 5.10). If prices are between the upper 1 standard

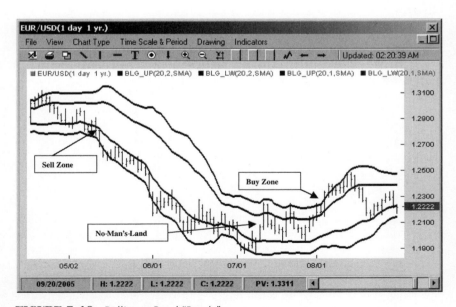

FIGURE 5.10 Bollinger Band "Bands"
Source: FXtrek IntelliChart™. Copyright 2001–2005 FXtrek.com, Inc.

deviation Bollinger band and the upper 2 standard deviation Bollinger band, they are in the buy zone. If a specific currency is trading between the lower 1 standard deviation Bollinger band and the lower 2 standard deviation band, then its price is in the sell zone. Price candles that exist in the area between the second Bollinger band "bands" are in effect in no-man's-land as markets struggle to find direction.

In essence, Bollinger band "bands" act as dynamic trend channels in a superior version of hand-drawn trend line channels covered earlier in this chapter. Because Bollinger bands are generated off the 20-period simple moving average, their readings can be mathematically calculated with a much better degree of accuracy than simple trend lines. Furthermore, the standard deviation formula naturally adapts to the volatility of price action, widening or narrowing the Bollinger channels accordingly.

For traders seeking a quick confirmation of trend, the Bollinger band "bands" approach offers an easy visual tool. One can use a variety of rules to trade with them, but I prefer the following simple rules. The example I will use refers to detecting and trading the uptrend (for the downtrend the rules are the same but simply reversed). To trade trend the trader needs to answer three basic questions:

1. *Trend detection*. When is a trend in place?
2. *Trade entry*. How is a position initiated?
3. *Trade exit*. What constitutes trend exhaustion?

With the Bollinger band "bands" approach, the trend detection rule is quite straightforward. I consider the uptrend to have commenced once the price closes—not simply penetrates, but closes—in the buy zone. The idea behind this rule is that buyers must have enough conviction behind their actions to sustain a rally into the upper Bollinger channel. If prices merely pierce the channel but cannot hold their value, then we do not have enough evidence of a clear up move in place.

The second component of the trade is perhaps the most tricky. Instead of simply entering the trade at market we will look for an opportunity to buy on any small dip into the no-man's-land zone. If the penetration of the buy zone is so powerful that prices reach the upper 2 standard deviation Bollinger band, then we will wait for prices to retrace to the middle of the bands or to the 1 standard deviation band. Why such hesitation? Shouldn't we just jump in the moment the trend becomes clear? No. Not if you want trade FX like a professional.

When it comes to trend trading in FX, the difference between professionals and amateurs is that while the pros are trend followers, the amateurs are trend chasers. The distinction may seem like nothing more than semantics, but in fact it's often what separates those who earn money through trading from those who lose it. But perhaps before I explain this point in more detail I should disclose the final component of the setup—the exit.

Where would the trader abandon his position? At what point on the chart will he be proven most likely wrong? If prices retreat all the way back to the lower 1 standard deviation Bollinger band, then the trader should stop out. The probability that trend is over is very high. Note the difference in approach. In order for us to consider the trend valid, prices must not only touch but close through the upper 1 standard deviation Bollinger band. As for our exit, a mere tag of the lower 1 standard deviation band will take us out of the trade. Why be so slow to enter and so quick to exit? Because, as I noted before, trend is not the common state of price, so price must really prove to the trader that it is making a directional move. Once price can't hold trend, there is absolutely no reason for the trend trader to stay around. His risks far outweigh potential rewards, because he now faces three possible scenarios—consolidation, trend reversal, or trend continuation. Two out of the three outcomes are unfavorable to his position and the last choice, which *is* advantageous, is usually the least likely under such circumstances.

Using the lower 1 standard deviation band provides ample room for the trend trader not to be falsely shaken out of the trade while the price meanders through the no-man's-land zone before it decides whether it wants to continue its initial impulse higher.

Understanding the exit—the third rule of the trade—may now be helpful to appreciating the second rule of buying only when the price retraces. It all has to do with risk and reward. Remember that in real life prices frequently fake out the trader. Just because price enters into the trend channel is no guarantee that it will remain there. If markets were highly predictable most traders would make money rather than lose it. The key to positioning in a trend-based setup is to minimize the amount of losses for the countless times you will inevitably be wrong, rather than to maximize the gains for the few times that you will be right. In trading, as I will never tire of stating, trends are the exception, not the rule, and in order to avoid being wiped out, traders need to try to always enter the market under the most advantageous of circumstances no matter what the market environment holds. Novice traders tend to succumb to the lure of the crowd and not restrain themselves from buying at the top or selling at the bottom. Note in Figure 5.11 how a trader who buys the high of the candle exposes himself to fully 300 points of losses in the GBP/USD trade as the uptrend fails and price retreats all the way to the lower Bollinger band. The more patient trader, however, who would wait for a retracement down to the upper 1 standard deviation Bollinger band,

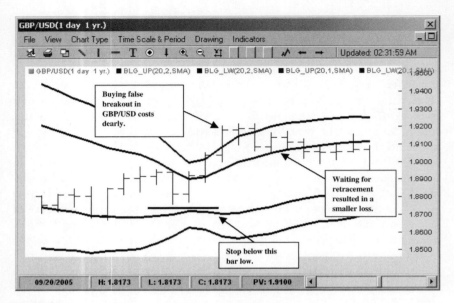

FIGURE 5.11 Buying on Retracement in GBP/USD
Source: FXtrek IntelliChart™. Copyright 2001–2005 FXtrek.com, Inc.

would suffer only a 150-point loss. Both trades are losers but one is less of a loss than the other.

Football fans know that the win does not necessarily go to the best athletic team but to the one that practices the best field management. Joe Theismann, the former quarterback for the Washington Redskins, once stated that he became a much better quarterback once he understood that he did not have to convert every third down play into the first down. If the opportunity just did not present itself to make first down, it was better to try for just a couple of extra yards, so the punter would have more room and could bury the opposition deeper in their own territory. Trading trend with Bollinger bands follows the same philosophy: When in the game the focus should always be on minimizing risk first, maximizing profit second.

In the example with the GBP/USD pair shown in Figure 5.12 the setup shows how well Bollinger bands can be used to trade trend with minimal risk. First the price enters into the sell zone, signaling the potential for a downward move. Second, it retraces back to the 1 standard deviation line, offering the trader a low-risk entry into the trade. If the trader is wrong he

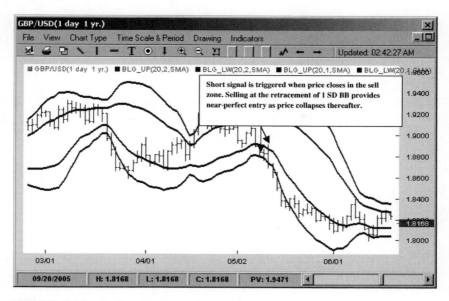

FIGURE 5.12 Trading Downtrend in GBP/USD
Source: FXtrek IntelliChart™. Copyright 2001–2005 FXtrek.com, Inc.

or she could stop out at the 20-period moving average, suffering only a minor loss. However, in this case the trader is correct and the profits turn out to be massive as the pair collapses for nearly 1,000 points of uninterrupted decline.

CONCLUSION

Contrary to popular opinion, identifying a trend is not nearly as difficult as it may seem. Whether we use trend lines, moving averages, Bollinger band "bands," or even, for some traders, the ADX, the technician's arsenal is full of tools capable of accurate trend analysis. Yet while detecting a trend is easy, trading it is not. By definition, all of the technical analysis indicators use past price data and are therefore highly vulnerable to whipsaws and fakeouts. No technical analysis tool can predict future price action. Indicators can only suggest it. Generally, the more specific the technical setup and the more the trader has thought through the variety of failures likely to befall it, the more robust the trade. In this chapter I have offered two setups (the compressed 3 SMA crossover and Bollinger band "bands") that not only utilize the basic tools of technical analysis but combine them in circumspect, logical ways to trade most traders' favorite price action—trend. In the next chapter we look at the far more common price behavior—range—and see how technical tools can help us to trade it successfully.

CHAPTER 6

Gauging Range

In the FX market, much as in life, most of the time nothing much happens. Prices meander back and forth as neither buyers nor sellers are able to make much progress. The rough estimate is that 70 to 80 percent of the time prices in the FX market stay in a range. Although these directionless price movements may bore some traders to tears, others build their whole livelihood on this fact. As I've discussed before, range trading requires a completely different set of skills and strategies than trend trading. Fortunately, technicians have a cornucopia of tools at their disposal to effectively analyze and properly trade range-bound markets. The class of indicators known as oscillators provides technically based traders with a set of very valuable clues to price action and helps them anticipate future price moves.

STOCHASTICS

Invented by Dr. George C. Lane, the tool known as stochastics is one of the oldest, yet one the most robust, technical oscillators around. Stochastics—with its Greek-derived name and its arcane parameter nomenclature—can at first glance appear rather obscure and difficult to understand. However, this tool is built on the basic technical premise that as prices rise in an uptrend, the close of each period will approach the high as bulls lift every offer, whereas in a downtrend the close will usually occur near the low as bears hit every bid.

79

Two measurements, which are normalized and bounded so that their values cycle from 0 to 100, make up stochastics. The first value, called %K, is calculated as follows:

$$\%K = 100 \times \frac{\text{Close at End of Period } n - \text{Low for Entire Period } n}{\text{High for Entire Period } n - \text{Low for Entire Period } n}$$

Typically the period n is set to 14.

The second measurement, called %D, is simply the three-period average of %K, which smooths out the moves of %K. %K and %D are awkward names for what are essentially two sets of moving averages that oscillate between 0 and 100. *Stochastic* is a term that refers to the location of the tradable's price relative to its range over the past 14 periods. So, for example, a stochastic reading of 55 simply means that the price is in the 55th percentile of its range or just about in the middle.

Fast and Slow

The stochastic indicator comes in two flavors: fast and slow. The formula for the fast stochastic was already presented. The slow stochastic, as the name implies, slows the stochastic indicator by replacing %K with its three-period simple moving average %D. The formula then calculates a new %D of this slower %K value. The idea is to smooth out even further the jumpiness of raw price data in order to ascertain the underlying trend.

Though relatively simple in concept, stochastics are the cornerstone for many technicians' range-bound setups because of their ability to gauge relatively oversold or overbought levels. The standard rule with stochastics is that a reading of 80 indicates that the tradable is overbought and a reading of 20 suggests an oversold price state. However, just because the currency pair is flashing a stochastic value of 80 does not mean that it cannot go materially higher in price, and similarly it can also decrease much further even if it prints a value below 20. In fact, during very strong uptrends stochastics may indicate a reading of 80 for many days, just as in a downtrend stochastic readings may dive down into the teens or even single digits. Dr. Lane was very clear that a stochastic of 80 does not mean that the trader must immediately short, nor does a reading of 20 mean that bids must be placed. Rather, the proper way to use stochastics is to observe the indicator once it has entered the overbought or oversold zone. Only when the indicator slips back below 80 or moves up above 20 does the trader follow the signal. Stochastics essentially measure momentum, and a break of the 80 line or a rally through the 20 line would indicate that buying or selling momentum has ceased and the trader is offered a high-probability directional trade (see Figure 6.1).

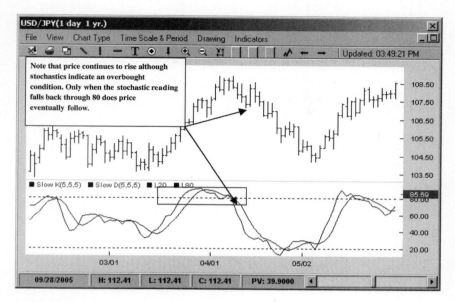

FIGURE 6.1 Trading with Stochastics
Source: FXtrek IntelliChart™. Copyright 2001–2005 FXtrek.com, Inc.

Divergence

George Lane contended that one of the most useful ways to utilize stochastics is by spotting divergence between the price action and the indicator readings. Specifically, he found the setup where the %D line would make lower highs while the price made higher highs a very useful short setup, and on the opposite side when the dynamic reversed itself with %D making higher lows while the price continued to make lower lows, this setup represented a potent long trade. He found that these types of trades were most reliable when divergence occurred as %D was between 10 and 15 on the downside and 85 and 90 on the upside (see Figure 6.2).

Stochastics are one of the earliest oscillator indicators and for that reason they have been abused by traders who misinterpret their signals. In highly range-bound markets, this tool *can* accurately call turns in price by simply flashing 80 or 20, but once the environment changes such simplistic trading will wreak havoc with your trading account, as price will continue to climb relentlessly against your shorts and fall against your longs. Stochastics are best used as a gauge of trend strength. Once trend weakens, stochastics will weaken as well. Even if price then resumes its prior direction, and even sets new highs in an uptrend or new lows in a

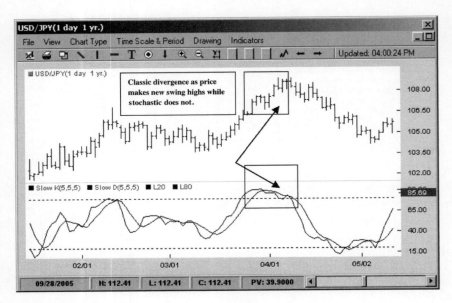

FIGURE 6.2 Trading Divergence with Stochastics
Source: FXtrek IntelliChart™. Copyright 2001–2005 FXtrek.com, Inc.

downtrend but stochastics do not confirm the price action, that piece of information could be of enormous value to the trader. Such a setup could signal the possible start of consolidation and range trading or a full-scale countertrend move. In either case, it's at this point that stochastics can offer the greatest value and the indicator can prove its mettle as one of the oldest albeit still valuable technical tools.

RELATIVE STRENGTH INDEX

Invented by master technician J. Welles Wilder, the Relative Strength Index (RSI) was first introduced in June 1978 in an article in *Futures* magazine. Since then, this indicator has become a mainstay of technical analysis, present in every single technical software package available on the market. In fact, if there was ever an indicator Hall of Fame, the RSI would no doubt be one of its founding members. The RSI, like stochastics, compares the strength of the currency pair to its price history. As an indicator it places more importance on recent price data and as such is very popular with currency traders who use it in a variety of ways. Because of its built-in smoothing functions, the RSI filters out the noise generated by spikes in price and is even used by some traders as a proxy for volume since volume reporting does not exist in FX.

The formula for the RSI is:

$$RSI = 100 - \frac{100}{1} + \frac{\text{Sum of Closes of Up Days / Entire Period } n}{\text{Sum of Closes of Down Days / Entire Period } n}$$

Typically the period n is set to 14.

Just like stochastics, the RSI is normalized and bounded so that it ranges from 0 to 100. The essence of the RSI is to measure the internal strength of the tradable by comparing the number of times that the currency pair is up in price versus the number of times that it is down in price over a given period of time. The classic setting for the RSI usually utilizes 14 periods, weighting the value of recent data by using the exponential averages for up days and down days to arrive at its final results. If the RSI registers readings above 70 the currency pair is considered to be overbought and if the reading is below 30 it is oversold. However, just as with stochastics, the simple fact that RSI reaches readings of 70 or 30 is not enough reason to suddenly sell or buy the pair. Rather it merely alerts the trader that price is now in an overbought or oversold state.

One of the most common methods of trading the RSI is by uncovering divergence patterns. If price is continually making new highs but the RSI does not, then a trend reversal or trend consolidation is highly likely (see Figure 6.3).

Because the RSI so effectively smooths price action, some traders even prefer to trade patterns off the RSI itself rather than off price action. In fact, a very strong argument can be made that trend lines and their concomitant breaks can be traded far more effectively off the RSI rather than off price action. Because price action, especially in the short term, can be highly volatile and unpredictable, it will often trigger numerous false signals and generate a large number of stop-outs for the trader. The RSI, in contrast, by smoothing out the price action may offer a truer picture of actual price direction (see Figure 6.4).

One interesting way to trade the RSI is as a proxy for the volume indicator. One of my colleagues, Adam Rosen, who serves as a senior Powercourse instructor at my firm, invented the following setup using the RSI to fade short-term spikes in the FX market. It is a trick he brought over from his days of prop trading New York Stock Exchange (NYSE) stocks using the volume indicator.

The rules of the setup are as follows. On an hourly chart look for

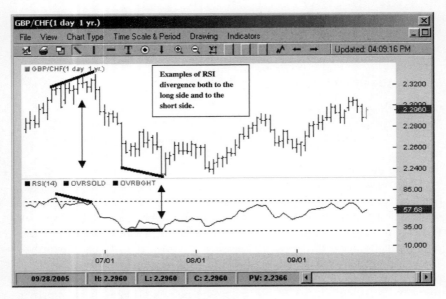

FIGURE 6.3 Trading Divergence Using RSI
Source: FXtrek IntelliChart™. Copyright 2001–2005 FXtrek.com, Inc.

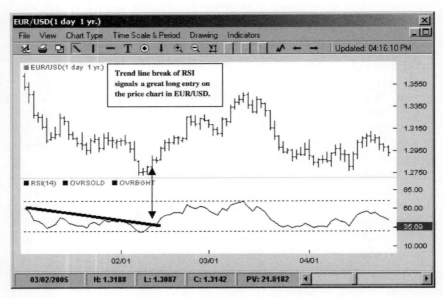

FIGURE 6.4 Trading Trend Lines on RSI Rather Than Price
Source: FXtrek IntelliChart™. Copyright 2001–2005 FXtrek.com, Inc.

readings of RSI 70 or higher or RSI 30 or lower to appear. Make sure that this reading occurs during the currency pair's active hours. The easiest way to define active hours for the currency pair is to use the stock market hours of each respective country as a time line guide. Since stock trading in each country is done during prime business hours, that would be defined as the active trading session for the currency pair. For some pairs this is actually a continuous time line of approximately 12 to 16 hours of the day, while for others active hours are comprised of two separate sessions during the 24-hour day. In the case of the EUR/USD, for example, the German DAX opens at 3 A.M. EST while the NYSE closes at 4 P.M. EST, so the active session for the EUR/USD is 3 A.M. until 4 P.M. EST. In the case of the USD/JPY, the Nikkei opens at 7 P.M. EST and closes as 3 A.M. with the NYSE then opening at 9:30 A.M. and closing at 4 P.M., so the active session for USD/JPY actually contains a gap in the time line. Table 6.1 provides active session times for the four major currency pairs and the three commodity pairs.

Once the price highs or price lows of the session are set and the RSI reading retreats from its oversold or overbought conditions and the active session hours are over, the trader would then measure the full amplitude (from the highs to the lows) of the active session range. The key factor in this setup is the RSI move off its extremes. If it maintains those levels, then the possibility of further price movement in the original direction is strong and the trader would stand aside. If the price rallied during the active session, then the trader would demarcate a sell zone at the top 20 percent of that day's range and further set a stop at 20 percent above the high

TABLE 6.1 Active Hours for Majors and Commodity Currencies

Pairs	Active Hours in Eastern Standard Time
EUR/USD	3:30 A.M.–4:00 P.M.
USD/JPY	9:30 P.M.–5:30 A.M. & 9:30 A.M.–4:00 P.M.
GBP/USD	4:30 A.M.–4:00 P.M.
USD/CHF	4:30 A.M.–4:00 P.M.
USD/CAD	9:30 A.M.–4:00 P.M.
AUD/USD	5:00 P.M.–12:00 A.M. & 9:30 A.M.–4:00 P.M.
NZD/USD	5:00 P.M.–12:00 A.M. & 9:30 A.M.–4:00 P.M.

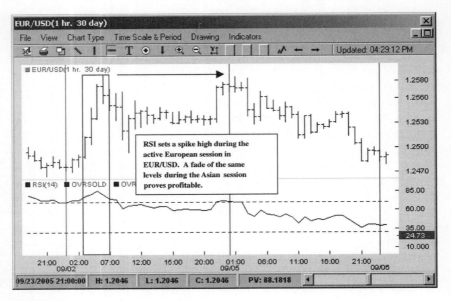

RSI sets a spike high during the active European session in EUR/USD. A fade of the same levels during the Asian session proves profitable.

FIGURE 6.5 RSI Fade in EUR/USD
Source: FXtrek IntelliChart™. Copyright 2001–2005 FXtrek.com, Inc.

of the range. As the price tries to retest the highs, the trader would short the move. Once the profit target reaches the same amount of points as risked on the trade, then half the position would be covered and the stop would be moved to break even. Figure 6.5 illustrates the RSI fade setup on the EUR/USD.

The RSI is one of the most robust oscillator tools in technical analysis. Its price-smoothing function frequently offers better clues to direction than price action itself. By applying trend line analysis right on the RSI itself, traders can generate accurate entry signals on both shorts and longs. Although ostensibly the indicator generates overbought or oversold signals, like all oscillators its real value is in spotting divergence between momentum and price.

One novel way that some traders have utilized the RSI in the currency market is as a proxy for volume. RSI readings above 70 and below 30 are equated to volume spikes seen in exchange-based markets and, depending on the immediate price action following those readings, can either be traded as trend-based volume breakouts or faded as signs of price exhaustion. Regardless of how one utilizes this tool, it is as versatile and as useful to a technically oriented trader as the Swiss army knife is to the traveling businessperson.

MOVING AVERAGE CONVERGENCE/DIVERGENCE

Is there a better indicator than the moving average convergence/divergence (MACD)? Some traders will assuredly say yes, of course there is. But for me the MACD is the most potent technical tool in my arsenal. In fact, I use the MACD and my Bollinger band "bands" to trade most of my setups in FX. The MACD is one of the simplest indicators around and is extremely versatile as it can be used both to gauge range as well as to trade trend.

Invented by Gerald Appel in 1978, the MACD is undoubtedly one of the top five most popular technical indicators in existence. Appel's brilliant insight was that as technicians we can learn more about price behavior from the *interaction* between moving averages than from the moving averages themselves. The MACD essentially plots the difference between the currency pair's 12-period and 26-period exponential moving averages. The idea is that if prices are rising, the 12-period exponential moving average (the faster moving average) will increase at a faster rate than the 26-period exponential moving average. The MACD therefore will slope upward. The reverse dynamic will occur if prices are falling. The MACD is an unbounded indicator, but it does oscillate around zero with readings becoming increasingly positive as prices rise and increasingly negative as they fall. One very simple method of trading the MACD is to buy when the MACD value turns positive and sell when it turns negative. Because the MACD records the difference between two moving averages rather than the moving averages themselves, it is far less prone to whipsaws as it filters out the periodic noise (see Figure 6.6).

The MACD is also plotted with its trigger line, which is simply the 9-period exponential moving average of the MACD itself. Much like the moving average crossover, the trigger line signal is traded when the MACD line crosses it from the upside or the downside. Because MACD calculations are naturally slower than the price action, these signals are always generated later than the price action itself. However, although these signals may be late they tend to be more accurate than mere moving average crossovers (see Figure 6.7).

In 1986 Thomas Aspray improved on Appel's original idea by inventing the MACD histogram, for me one of the most useful technical tools in existence. The histogram is simply the visual representation of the difference between the MACD line and its trigger line, but its real value rests on the fact that it is a very effective momentum indicator. The MACD histogram oscillates around the zero line, which is the point at which the MACD and the trigger line cross each other. When prices rise, the MACD will tend to pull away from its trigger line, as the most recent values will cause the MACD to increase at a faster rate than its 9-period EMA.

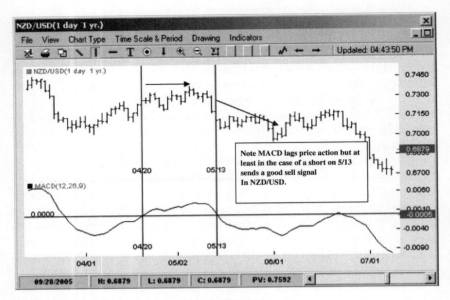

FIGURE 6.6 MACD Zero Line Crossover in NZD/USD
Source: FXtrek IntelliChart™. Copyright 2001–2005 FXtrek.com, Inc.

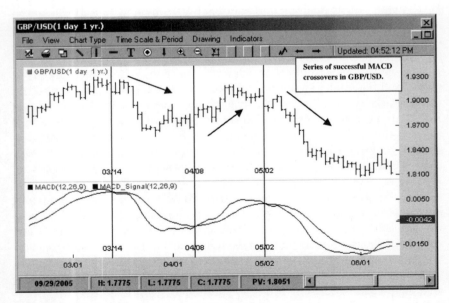

FIGURE 6.7 MACD Crossovers in GBP/USD
Source: FXtrek IntelliChart™. Copyright 2001–2005 FXtrek.com, Inc.

At its core, the MACD histogram measures the velocity of price movement, which can offer a technically oriented trader a very strong clue to future price action. The key technical concept, in fact the essence of all technical analysis, is that changes in momentum precede changes in price. The concept is actually eminently reasonable if we just think for a moment of what happens during a strong directional move.

Let's imagine that prices are in an uptrend. Buyers have bid the currency pair up, making higher highs. Typically price action will have the following pattern: First prices will break out as early buyers pile into the currency in anticipation of a rise. Then more traders seeing the rise in the currency will join the price action in hopes of extending the trend. Additionally, short sellers who are now deep in loss territory will begin to cover as they realize that they are on the wrong side of the market. This reaction will only fuel prices higher and then Johnny-come-lately buyers will jump on the trend bandwagon, believing that prices will continue their linear progression. At this point most of the players who wanted to buy have already established their positions and the rate of new highs slows. The early buyers who have now amassed substantial profits begin to liquidate their positions as they see prices level off. All of this jockeying translates into one simple fact: Velocity has slowed markedly. If at the beginning of the trend it took only five minutes to move prices higher by 50 points, now it may take several hours to move them only 2 or 3 points higher, or worse yet they may actually begin to decline as early winners take profits while there are no additional buyers to absorb their sells.

The MACD histogram is a very sensitive measure of price velocity and as such is a very useful tool in one of my favorite setups—the MACD turn. The MACD turn essentially trades the MACD histogram rather than the price action itself. A buy signal is generated once the MACD histogram makes a peak. In the case of a long signal the MACD histogram would need to record a higher low on one of its bars. The trader would then assume a long position (see Figure 6.8 for a sell signal). Note that very frequently the price will continue to decline even as the MACD histogram posts higher lows. Most traders will panic at this point and will stop themselves out, typically just at absolute price lows. This is almost always a critical mistake. One of the key tenets of trading with indicators is that the trader should stay with the logic of his setup. If the entry was based on an indicator signal, then the stop-exit should be based on the indicator as well. In the MACD turn example I would stop myself out of the trade only if the MACD value made a new swing low. In the MACD turn trade the trick is to trade the indicator, not the price.

Many novice technical traders will enter on an indicator signal but will exit on some predetermined price. This in fact is the trading equiva-

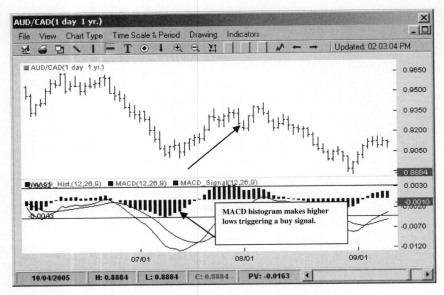

FIGURE 6.8   Trading the MACD Histogram in AUD/CAD
Source: FXtrek IntelliChart™. Copyright 2001–2005 FXtrek.com, Inc.

lent of comparing apples and oranges. There is little logic in such a setup and it will frequently fail as result. Little wonder, then, that many traders who experiment with indicators quickly give up in frustration and proclaim that technical analysis "does not work." That certainly is true; any set of tools utilized incorrectly will fail at their intended task. However, the most difficult notion to understand about a technical analysis tool like MACD is that even when they are used properly they can fail as well.

The basis of technical analysis is that momentum precedes price. That means failure in momentum will occur before failure in price. In a declining market, momentum will usually taper off before price will stop decreasing. Generally, this is a very high-probability bet. On some occasions, however, momentum will send a fake signal. Note in Figure 6.9 how the MACD initially turns upward suggesting that momentum is increasing but then quickly reverts back. At that point it is critical for the trader to stop himself out because his key criterion—positive momentum in the form of an ever-increasing MACD histogram slope—has been negated.

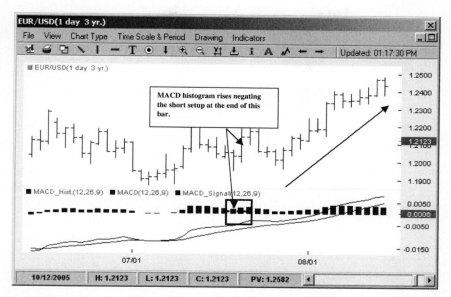

FIGURE 6.9 Stopping Out of a Short as MACD Turns Positive
Source: FXtrek IntelliChart™. Copyright 2001–2005 FXtrek.com, Inc.

COMMODITY CHANNEL INDEX

The Commodity Channel Index (CCI), invented by Donald Lambert in 1980, was originally designed to solve engineering problems regarding signals. The indicator was adapted for trading of commodities and later popularized by Ken Wood, who used it to trade a variety of financial instruments, including currency futures.

Donald Lambert's intent in developing the CCI was to manufacture an indicator that would try to normalize momentum readings. Like stochastics and RSI, the prime focus of the CCI is to measure the deviation of the price of the tradable from its statistical average. The CCI uses several sophisticated tricks to achieve its goal. Instead of simply taking the closing price reading over a specific period, the formula for the CCI calculates what Lambert calls the typical price, which is in fact the average of the high, low, and close. The net effect of that calculation is that the typical price is more representative of the whole array of the prices during that period rather than just the close. The typical price then subtracts the average of typical prices over a number of periods—usually 14. This numerator is then divided by the mean deviation of this result multiplied by a constant 0.15.

Mathematically the formula looks like this:

1. Calculate the last period's typical price (TP) = (H + L + C)/3 where H = high, L = low, and C = close.

2. Calculate the 20-period simple moving average of the typical price (SMATP).

3. Calculate the mean deviation. First, calculate the absolute value of the difference between the last period's SMATP and the typical price for each of the past 20 periods. Add all of these absolute values together and divide by 20 to find the mean deviation.

4. The final step is to apply the typical price (TP), the simple moving average of the typical price (SMATP), a constant (0.015), and the mean deviation to the following formula:

$$CCI = \text{Typical Price} - \frac{\text{SMATP}}{0.015} \times \text{Mean Deviation}$$

In essence, the CCI is simply a measure of divergence from the SMA, which is constantly normalized in relation to the volatility of price flow. The CCI, like the MACD, generates positive and negative values. The assumption behind its design is that between 70 to 80 percent of all prices will fall between CCI readings of +100 and –100. The classic way to read the CCI is that prices become overbought when they exceed +100 and oversold when they decline below –100. However, the standard way to trade the CCI is not to fade price flow when those readings are reached but to actually go with it. Traders should buy the currency when the CCI breaks above +100 and sell it when it falls below –100. For traders wishing to fade price flow, the recommendation is to wait until the price leaves the +100 zone to initiate sells (see Figure 6.10), and the reverse—to wait until it pokes above the –100 zone—to initiate buys. Much like with stochastics and RSI, the process of fading strength and weakness is twofold: First the price must create overbought or oversold conditions by piercing the +/–100 zones and then it must leave them. The drawback of such an approach is that the trader is frequently late to the turn. Because the CCI continuously produces its reading from what is essentially a derivative of a derivative (moving average of a moving average), the signal will almost always be triggered after the price has made part of its move. However, the value of this more cautious approach is that traders do not put themselves into the position of shorting an ever-rising market or buying an

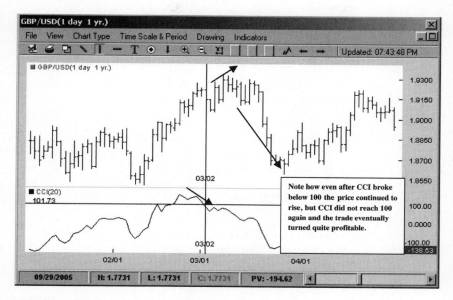

FIGURE 6.10 Trading with CCI in GBP/USD
Source: FXtrek IntelliChart™. Copyright 2001–2005 FXtrek.com, Inc.

ever-falling one, as CCI values could remain in highly overbought or over-sold states for a long period of time.

Like all moving average–derived indicators, the CCI of course is subject to whipsaw risk as it can dart in and out of the +/–100 zones several times before settling on direction. For this reason many traders prefer to use the CCI as a divergence indicator. If the price continues to make higher highs but the CCI makes lower highs within the +100 zone, a trader may consider initiating a short position and maintain that short position even if the price continues to make newer highs as long as the CCI does not exceed its prior highs (see Figure 6.11). The setup of course works exactly the same way in reverse with the CCI making higher lows while the price proceeds to decline.

One novel way of trading the CCI has emerged from Ken Wood, universally known as Woodie to his many legions of fans and fellow traders. Woodie hosts more than 10 separate trading chat groups on the Internet where he and his followers trade a variety of financial instruments including currency futures in the EUR/USD using the CCI exclusively as their indicator of choice.

In an interview with *SFO* magazine Ken Wood stated, "Many years ago, right after the CCI article appeared, I was doing work on momentum—because I always found that for some reason momentum gave a

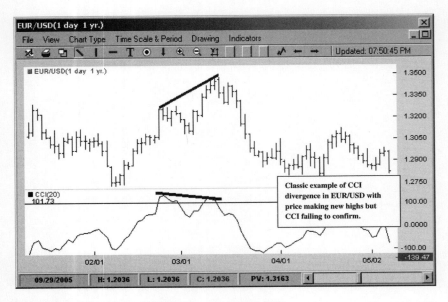

FIGURE 6.11 Trading CCI Divergence in EUR/USD
Source: FXtrek IntelliChart™. Copyright 2001–2005 FXtrek.com, Inc.

little bit of a warning ahead of time of what was going to happen. And the CCI is classified as a momentum indicator. I began using the CCI and started to develop patterns on it about 13 to 14 years ago; I noticed that these particular patterns were continuously showing up on daily charts at that time—all the time. And so, that's when I started developing the patterns on the CCI and not on the price bars." That indeed was Woodie's great insight and contribution to technical analysis. Instead of trading price charts, Woodie trades the classic technical patterns that form on the CCI. Since the CCI is specifically designed to normalize price data, this method protects Woodie from the random market noise of pure price action. Woodie in fact sets up his charts without any price axis whatsoever so that he can simply concentrate on the patterns formed by the CCI and not be swayed by the price action itself. That's an act of mental discipline few traders could practice, but the underlying core of his philosophy— trade the indicator, not the price—has been a tremendous insight and help to many technically oriented traders. Indeed, I borrowed this concept in designing my MACD turn setup.

Among Woodie's most popular CCI setups are the ghost, the trend line break, and the zero line reject patterns. The ghost pattern, though rare, can be a very powerful trade. The ghost is simply the head and shoulders pattern on the CCI itself, which suggests that momentum has made a peak and a price reversal may soon follow. It is especially useful in timing a turn in price after a long trend period. Note in Figure 6.12 how the ghost setup warned traders of an impending trend change in the EUR/USD after the price had climbed 1,000 points.

The trend line break simply uses a break of trend line on the CCI rather than price to trigger a trade. The trend line break can be a very powerful setup, especially if it is combined with the cross of the zero line. Again, because the CCI normalizes the price data, its peaks and valleys will be smoother and less random than the price itself; therefore, a break of trend as mapped by the CCI will have more meaning and accuracy than trend line breaks on price charts alone.

Finally, one other common setup of Woodie's is the zero line reject, where the CCI approaches the zero line (though many traders use the 0–50 zone for more flexibility) and then begins to turn away. The trader would quickly buy the currency pair in the case of a positive zero line reject trade and sell it in the case of a negative zero line reject trade (see Figure 6.13). The exit for the trade would occur when the CCI reading exceeded 100 or –100. This in effect is a classic retracement trade where the trader buys weakness in the uptrend and sells strength in a downtrend, and then quickly exits at the extremes. The difference is that using the

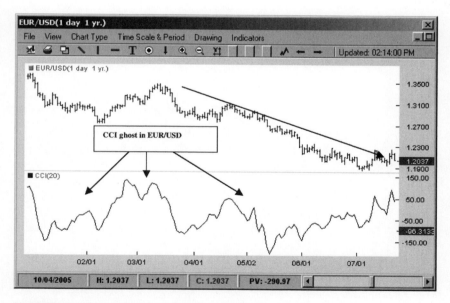

FIGURE 6.12 Trading CCI "Ghost" in EUR/USD
Source: FXtrek IntelliChart™. Copyright 2001–2005 FXtrek.com, Inc.

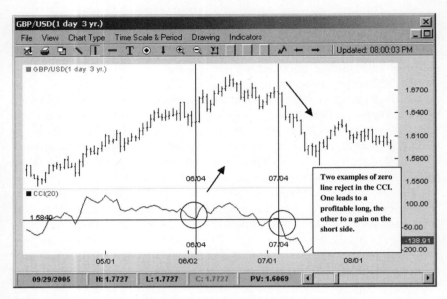

FIGURE 6.13   Trading CCI Zero Line Reject in GBP/USD
Source: FXtrek IntelliChart™. Copyright 2001–2005 FXtrek.com, Inc.

CCI provides the trader with a very precise framework to execute this strategy.

CONCLUSION

Ultimately all oscillators simply measure the rate of change in price action. Their formulas may differ and their readings may have slight variability, but their primary usefulness to a technician is to spot divergence between momentum and price. Does a break in momentum always predict a turn in price? Of course not. In fact, such primitive application of oscillators is precisely the reason why many novice traders are unable to benefit from technical analysis. One of the principal tenets of successful technical trading is to maintain a logical structure to one's trading setups. Traders should trade either indicators or price action but not mix the two.

Indicator signals are only clues, not guarantees about future price direction. Those technical traders who focus strictly on analyzing and trading indicators will have a much greater degree of success because their trade setups will possess an inherent logical structure.

Like all rules in life, the one I just stated needs to be broken occasionally. All technical indicators by definition lag price action because they are composed of past price history. Furthermore, because many oscillators normalize the price data, their signals may be even further delayed. In case of extraordinary volatility, trading strictly off indicators may create highly damaging and perhaps even fatal drawdowns to account equity. Traders always need to have a disaster response scenario before they put on a trade that requires a hard money stop, regardless of what indicators say.

Oscillators are the primary tools of technical analysis because most technical analysis is centered on the concept of divergence between momentum and price. They, like all tools in technical analysis, are not by any scientific means precise. However, used properly they can offer a critical edge to the trader, and in a business where one needs to be only 51 percent correct on an even risk/reward basis, that is a valuable service indeed.

CHAPTER 7

Fibs Don't Fib

L eonardo of Pisa, who lived from 1170 to 1250 and is better known as Fibonacci, is the most popular mathematician in trading, more famous even than Fischer Black and Myron Scholes, who invented the Black-Scholes formula, which is the foundation for all modern pricing of options. Fibonacci's contribution was far less complex than the Black-Scholes option pricing model. He is best known to traders for discovering the sequence of numbers that carries his name. The sequence proceeds like this: 0, 1, 1, 2, 3, 5, 8, 13, 21, 34, 55, 89, 144, 233, 377, 610, 987, 1597, and so on. The series is constructed by choosing the first two numbers, known as the seeds, and then constructing the next number from the sum of the two prior numbers. The Fibonacci sequence obeys the formula $P(n) = P(n - 1) + P(n - 2)$ and is an example of many such sequences in mathematics known as recursion relations.

The Fibonacci sequence has several neat mathematical properties, including:

1. If you take any three adjacent numbers, then square the middle number and multiply the two outside numbers, the difference between those two values will always be 1.
2. If you take any four adjacent numbers, then multiply the two outside numbers and multiply the two inside numbers, the product of the two outside numbers will always be 1 more or 1 less than the product of the inside numbers.

3. Finally, the sum of any 10 adjacent numbers will always be equal to the value of multiplying the seventh number of that sequence by 11.

While these tricks are mildly amusing, in trading the Fibonacci sequence is revered for the fact that the ratio of adjacent numbers converges to a constant value of 0.618. Note this not the case for the smaller numbers—as for example 2:3 is equal to 0.66 and 5:8 is equal to 0.625—but as numbers progress, especially as the sequence exceeds about 55 numbers, the ratio of each adjacent number begins to equal 0.618 all the way to the tenth decimal point. This ratio is often referred to as "phi." The other quite interesting aspect of the Fibonacci sequence is that the reciprocal of that ratio is equal to 1.618 or 1 + phi. In other words, 144/233 = 0.618 and 233/144 = 1.618. This remarkable property is consistent throughout the sequence.

Is the Fibonacci sequence unique? Not at all. As mentioned, it's part of a family of mathematical series called recursive relations. Another famous series is called the Lucas sequence, after French mathematician Edouard Lucas (1842–1891), which is "seeded" with 1 and 3 instead of 0 and 1. The Lucas sequence has the following string: 1, 3, 4, 7, 11, 18, 29, 47, and so on. As its numbers increase, its ratio also approaches phi. No other sequence, though, with different seed numbers and different summation rules will converge to phi. For example, a sequence with seed values 0, 1, 1 and the summary rules changed so that $P(n) = P(n-2) + P(n-3)$ will generate the series 0, 1, 1, 2, 2, 3, 4, 5, 7, 9, and so on. The ratio of the two adjacent numbers will converge to 0.754, and the reciprocal value will be 1.32—quite different from Fibonacci values. However, the one property that all of these recursive series share is that the ratios of their adjacent numbers quickly converge to nearly constant values. After about 30 generations the ratio numbers become constant to 10 decimal points.

So what's all the fuss about? Why are Fibonacci ratios so important? To their proponents "Fibs" hold almost mystical values. Petals of flowers, planetary orbits, and human physiology all adhere to this ratio. If the Fibonacci sequence and its ratio are so widespread in nature, then they reason it should have powerful application to the financial markets, which, after all, are a reflection of natural human behavior. Like many traders, I used to accept this line of reasoning without question until I came across a critique of the whole Fibonacci philosophy by Donald Simanek, a professor at Lock Haven University of Pennsylvania and author of *Science Askew* (Institute of Physics Publishing, 2001). Professor Simanek eviscerates the whole "Fibonacci is the key to natural order" argument by pointing out the inconsistencies in the adherents' positions. For example, on the matter of flowers the proponents argue that petals follow the Fibonacci sequence. Table 7.1 lists all such flowers.

TABLE 7.1 Petal Numbers That Are "Fibs"

Flower	Number of Petals
Lily	3
Violet	5
Delphinium	8
Mayweed	13
Aster	21
Pyrethrum	34
Helenium	55
Michaelmas Daisy	89

The problem is that this list is selective. There are plenty of flowers whose petals are not Fibonacci numbers. Professor Simanek points out just a few such examples in Table 7.2.

Similarly, the orbital rotations of Uranus, Saturn, Jupiter, and Mars happen to follow the Fibonacci ratio when a planet's period is compared to the planet adjacent to it. However, as Professor Simanek points out, the orbits of Pluto, Neptune, Venus, and Earth do not, making the whole process rather subjective and arbitrary.

Finally on the question of human physiology many Fibonacci adherents claim that perfect human features both on the face and on the body will follow the Fib ratio. One very often quoted Fib concept is that the perfect human body will have a "phi" relationship between the height of the person's navel as measured from the floor relative to the person's full height. Professor Simanek actually tested this assertion by measuring a large sample of swimsuit models deemed beautiful by most standards and

TABLE 7.2 Petal Numbers That Are Not "Fibs"

Flower	Number of Petals
Mustard	4
Dame's Rocket	4
Hyacinth	6
Corn Lily	6
Solomon's Seal	6
Starflower	7

arrived at an average of 0.58 with a variance of only +/–.01 versus the phi ratio of 0.62.

So where does all of this leave us? Are the claims of Fib proponents that this sequence has critical value to understanding the order of the universe complete nonsense? Absolutely. Are Fibonacci ratios therefore completely useless when applied to currency trading? Absolutely not.

In the FX markets Fibonacci ratios are keenly observed. The key Fibonacci levels that most traders follow are 0.382 percent (1 minus "phi" ratio of 0.618), 50 percent (which is not a true Fibonacci ratio and already shows a perversion of the dogma), and phi itself (0.618). Additionally, traders also key in on what are called Fibonacci extension ratios—1.382 and 1.618. The classic way to apply the Fib ratios in technical analysis is to draw a trend line from the absolute swing low to the absolute swing high in an uptrend (reverse in a downtrend) and then to attach Fib lines at 38.2 percent, 50 percent, and 61.8 percent levels of the move. The idea is that prices will correct by these amounts in any type of trend as these are natural support and resistance levels (see Figures 7.1 and 7.2).

For Fib extensions the process also relies on marking the near-term length of the trend but then simply multiplying that value by 1.382 and 1.618 to project the key levels that prices are likely to reach (see Figure

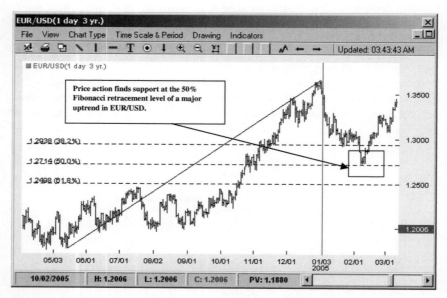

FIGURE 7.1 Finding Support with Fibonacci in EUR/USD
Source: FXtrek IntelliChart™. Copyright 2001–2005 FXtrek.com, Inc.

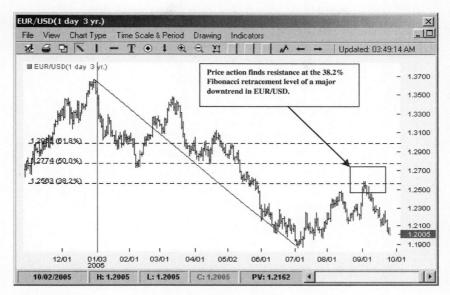

FIGURE 7.2 Determining Resistance with Fibonacci in EUR/USD
Source: FXtrek IntelliChart™. Copyright 2001–2005 FXtrek.com, Inc.

7.3). For example, in the case of an uptrend in EUR/USD from a swing low of 1.2000 to a swing high of 1.2100 a Fibonacci-based trader would demarcate the length of the trend as 100 points and would project 1.2138 as his first point of exit and 1.2162 as his second profit target.

Why use Fibonacci ratios at all in trading if they are of dubious merit scientifically? Part of the reason is that almost everyone in the FX market—from the smallest speculator in Spokane, Washington, to the largest hedge fund trader in Greenwich, Connecticut—is aware of these levels. The process is only reinforced by the financial press, which disseminates the information on Fib levels through almost every FX web site on the Internet. The fact that these numbers are well known and that market participants follow them avidly makes Fib levels a useful reference tool. However, ultimately I think this is a weak argument in the vein of "Well I did it because everyone was doing it, too."

There is, I believe, a better and more logical reason for why Fib levels work quite well in the currency market. Stripped of their mystical nonsense, the Fib ratios basically represent proportions of about one-third and two-thirds of the total value of the move. To understand why these are natural retrenchment levels for currencies we need to examine the basic dynamics of trading. In a trending market, when prices find direction FX

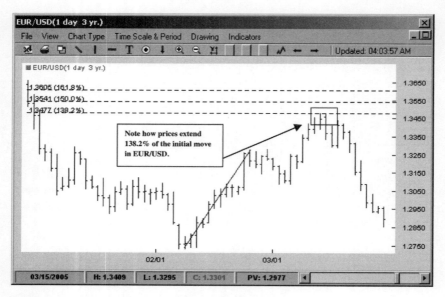

FIGURE 7.3   Fibonacci Extensions in EUR/USD
Source: FXtrek IntelliChart™. Copyright 2001–2005 FXtrek.com, Inc.

dealers can typically be found on the opposite side of the move. This result is the natural outcome of the dealers' function as market makers. When customers come to buy they must be willing to sell in order to provide liquidity to the market. Unlike customers, dealers almost never put on their whole position at once. Instead they continuously scale in and out of their positions, riding the price charts, absorbing and removing inventory much like a fast elevator in a high-rise building. As prices continue to move in one direction, dealers and other short-term market speculators may begin to parabolically scale into their positions. Simply put, they may start not just to average up but to double up at each new high or low. This method may appear to be financially suicidal, and for most speculators with limited capital it certainly would be. But for large-scale traders with access to enormous credit lines and seasoned experience with risk, this strategy can be highly efficient. Let's just look at a hypothetical example to see the real dynamic at play.

Imagine that EUR/USD is trading at 1.2000. Dealer X as part of his market making duties sells 100 million euros to his customers. An unexpected piece of news hits the market and the EUR/USD jumps to 1.2100. Most market participants on the wrong side of that trade may choose to cover for a loss and get out at that point. But remember our Dealer X has spent only a fraction of his total available capital on that position and may decide to stay with the position. At 1.2100 he will sell 200 million euros more into the market. The EUR/USD rally, however, continues to build steam and the pair now trades at 1.2200. At this point even the most steely-eyed short-term speculator is likely to cover as the pain of the loss becomes nearly unbearable. Our Dealer X, however, still has plenty of capital in reserve and chooses to sell once again—this time 400 million euros at 1.2200. As prices move uninterrupted for 200 points in one direction the early winners from this trade—the longs who have been in since 1.2000—may decide to cash in some of their positions. Focus, however, on our friend Dealer X. What has he really done? Essentially he has lowered his break-even point by two-thirds of the amplitude of the move. Or put differently, prices have to retrace by only one-third in order for Dealer X's position to become profitable: (100 million × 1.2000) + (200 million × 1.2100) + (400 million × 1.2200) = average price of 1.12142.

In parabolic averaging, where the trader always doubles up his positions at any given interval, the break-even point will be one-third of the length of the move. Of course, the preceding is an idealized example. Nobody continuously doubles up their positions ad infinitum. Such a system would be simply nothing but a version of the martingale technique where the gambler repeatedly doubles his bet until he can recoup his original capital. All martingale systems are doomed to fail eventually. However, unlike what you may have read in trading books, in real life professional traders often double down on their positions in a modified version of the martingale technique. There are two key differences between the pros and the amateurs. First, professionals almost never spend all of their risk capital on a single entry. Note that in our example Dealer X may have had as much as a billion euros of credit available to him, and even with all of the doubling his total trade allocation was only 700 million euros. Second, professionals always set an exit point for a trade gone wrong even if it's a very wide emergency stop hundreds of points away. Unlike the amateur martingale gamblers who tempt fate once too often and will inevitably lose all of their capital, pros always cut their losses at a small percentage of their overall capital.

Is it any wonder, then, that the 38.2 percent Fib level seems to resonate in currency trading? This is the first zone at which traders trapped on the wrong side of the move are able to get out of their positions at break-even or better. As prices approach these levels, these players would become natural sellers if the original move was a downtrend or natural buyers if it was an uptrend. Therefore, just as the early speculators on the right side of the trend who wanted to cash out their winnings presented a natural barrier to any further directional move, so, too, these countertrend traders now present a natural cap to any retracement.

Is it the mysterious power of Fibonacci or is it simply the natural ebb and flow of the markets that makes the main Fibonacci retracement levels so valuable in FX trading? I would strongly argue that it's the latter. But you may wonder, why care either way? After all, if Fib levels work in FX, why not simply use them profitably regardless of the reasons for their efficacy? Because it's important not to accord too much meaning to Fibonacci numbers. Very rarely do prices make an exact 38.2 percent retracement and then immediately turn back.The Fib retracement ratios are not some precise mathematical calculations that allow the trader to anticipate support and resistance levels with the same degree of certainty that allows NASA engineers to land a spaceship on the moon. On the contrary, traders who try to anticipate the Fibonacci retracement level are often disappointed as prices run over their positions before finally making a turn. Although on occasion it may be quite profitable to simply put in a limit order at the 38.2 percent or 61.8 percent level, catch the absolute bottom of the retracement, and then watch as prices bounce right off that level to resume their original direction, in real life such setups have a very low probability of success. Far better for most traders to observe price action as it actually meets Fibonacci levels. Typically if the Fib support is real, the velocity of the move will slow down and prices may spend several periods consolidating in that region. If prices then resume the original trend, the trader may have more confidence that the Fib support level is genuine, and his trade, though far from certain, would have a higher probability of success (see Figure 7.4).

Fib levels are not static, rigid lines that serve as inviolable support for any given trend; rather, they are more like elastic rubber bands that dynamically absorb price action in a broad zone before the price resumes its original move. Dennis Gartman, who writes the eponymous newsletter that covers the currency, stock, bond, and commodity markets and is read the world over by most institutional traders, uses what he calls the "box" to gauge retracement levels in a trend. The box is simply the 50 percent to 61.8 percent zone of any given trend (see Figure 7.5). Gartman likes to see how prices react when they enter into the box; if they stall he will often place a trade in the direction of the original trend, betting that the retracement is over. Note that instead of relying on specific numerical lines, Gartman uses a wide area of price action as his measure of support. Fibonacci levels become important not in their ability to pinpoint specific retracement levels, but rather in the utility to point out the broad general areas of support and resistance that should hold if the original trend is to resume pace.

Besides acting as zones of support, Fibonacci levels also offer higher-probability trades when multiple Fibonacci retracement lines converge on a single value. Known as Fib confluence, this dynamic occurs when Fibonacci

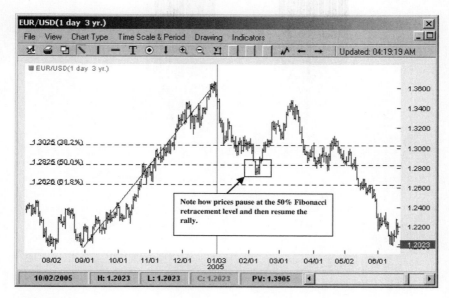

FIGURE 7.4 Confirming Fibonacci Support in EUR/USD
Source: FXtrek IntelliChart™. Copyright 2001–2005 FXtrek.com, Inc.

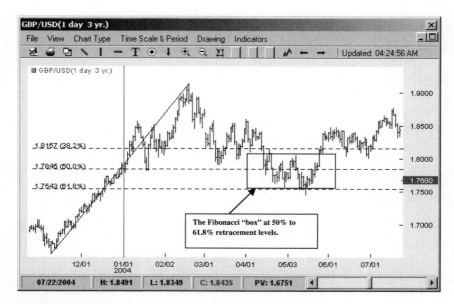

FIGURE 7.5 Trading the Fibonacci "Box" in GBP/USD
Source: FXtrek IntelliChart™. Copyright 2001–2005 FXtrek.com, Inc.

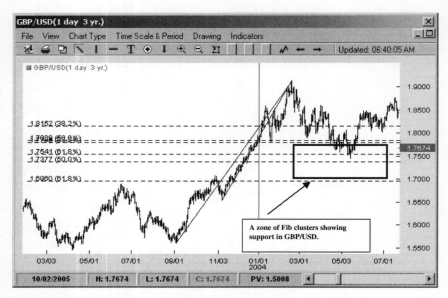

FIGURE 7.6 Trading Support at Fib Clusters in GBP/USD
Source: FXtrek IntelliChart™. Copyright 2001–2005 FXtrek.com, Inc.

support or resistance lines on, say, an hourly trend, a daily trend, and a weekly trend all approach the same level. As prices reach this intersection of support or resistance for multiple moves, technical analysis will consider it far more valid as traders from all time horizons (the short-term speculators, the intermediate-term swing traders, and the long-term position traders) will all have reason to sell or buy at that point. Note how in Figure 7.6 the Fibonacci confluence puts an iron lid on the rally in GBP/USD as multiple Fibonacci retrace lines vector in on the 1.9000 level.

TRADING BREAKOUT AND RETRACEMENT WITH FIBONACCI

One of Fibonacci's most useful properties is that it can be used effectively to trade both trend continuation and trend retracement (see Figures 7.7 and 7.8). Because trend trading is usually a more common technique for most traders, let's take a look at that approach first.

Imagine that the EUR/USD pair makes a strong breakout on the hourly charts. Although it's impossible to be certain that the move will follow through, a trend trader would go long in anticipation of further upside

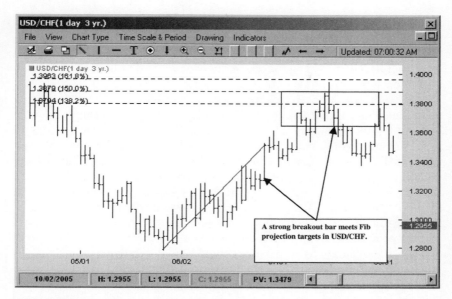

FIGURE 7.7 Projecting Breakout Targets with Fibonacci
Source: FXtrek IntelliChart™. Copyright 2001–2005 FXtrek.com, Inc.

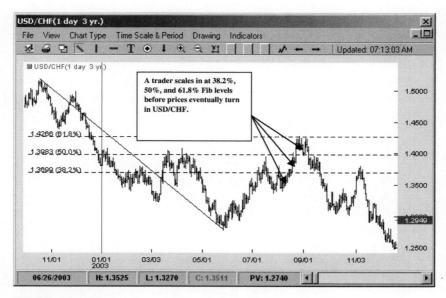

FIGURE 7.8 Scaling into Trade Using Fibonacci Levels
Source: FXtrek IntelliChart™. Copyright 2001–2005 FXtrek.com, Inc.

price movement. In fact, most breakouts will usually fail, but because it is impossible to know which breakouts will succeed and which ones will fail, trend traders have to take every trade. As the saying goes, "You have to be in it to win it." Using Fibonacci, however, breakout traders can optimize their few wins while minimizing their many losses.

To trade the breakout setup properly, you could use the following technique: Once the breakout candle prints, enter at market but with only half your total trade size. If you are correct and the price continues to move in your favor, you can add a quarter more at 138.2 percent of the initial breakout move. Finally, if the trade momentum persists you can add the final 25 percent of the position at 161.8 percent of the move.

This strategy is a variation of an idea presented by Josh Lukeman in his book *The Market Maker's Edge* (McGraw-Hill, 2003) and is known as pressing the trade. Using Fibonacci levels as his guideposts the trader carefully increases his position as price action moves his way. Let's look at a specific example to better understand how the trade works.

Imagine that the length of the breakout candle is 100 pips long and it closes on the high at 1.3300. Your total capital budget for the trade is 200,000 units or two standard lots. To properly execute this setup you would take the following steps:

1. Buy 100,000 units (one lot) at 1.3300 and place a stop-loss order at 1.3260, 40 points underneath the entry price. This is a rather tight stop just below the first 38.2 percent Fibonacci retracement level. However, the motto of the breakout trader is "Either I am right or I am out!" If prices retrace much more than the first Fib level, the case for a momentum-based move would be greatly diluted and the probability for success diminished. If prices do retrace that far, you would lose 40 points but only on half of your intended position, so the net loss would be only 20 points.

2. If, however, prices continue to trend, you would add another 50,000 units (half lot) at 1.3338, which would be equal to the 138.2 percent Fibonacci projection of the move. Your average cost would now stand at 1.3312. You could then tighten the stop to 1.3298, just below the 38.2 percent retracement level, consistent with the logic that a trend move should maintain momentum. Again, if the trade is stopped out you would lose only 20 points.

3. As the price continues to move higher you would add the final 50,000 units to the position at the 162.8 percent Fib projection level, which would be equal to 1.3363. Having put on the full position, your average cost now stands at 1.3325. If the price reaches your target of 1.3400 you will now have 75 points of reward for the maximum 25 points of risk.

This approach has several advantages. First and foremost, it minimizes risk by committing only half your capital at the beginning of the trade. Using Fibonacci levels as your guideposts you are then able to add 50 percent more capital to the trade without materially increasing your average cost. Instead of costing 1.3300, the trade cost rises to only 1.3325 and only after the price action confirms the breakout bias, making the trade much more likely to become profitable. The net result is that the trade now posseses very favorable risk/reward characteristics of 3:1, which are crucial for long-term success of breakout-based traders since the strategy is generally fraught with failure and fakeouts, even in a highly trending market like FX. Therefore, even if the trader is successful only 40 times out of 100, given such favorable payoff he would have a positive expectancy and should be able to generate a profit in the long run.

Now let's take a look at a reverse situation and see how Fib ratios can help the trader to properly position himself for a retracement trade. Imagine the same breakout scenario where prices rise from 1.3200 to 1.3300 except you are less confident in believing that prices will immediately continue forward but are still convinced that they will ultimately rise. Again you budget 200,000 units of the EUR/USD for the trade, but here is how you would set up the trade to maximize your chances of success.

1. Buy 50,000 units (25 percent of total position) at 1.3300 (initial entry level). If you are wrong and the price continues its upward direction right away you would at least participate in the move with a partial position targeting the 1.3400 exit.

2. Buy another 50,000 units (you will now have fully 50 percent of your position) at 1.3262 (38.2 percent Fib retracement of the candle). If the price now bounces off the Fib support you will have 50 percent of your position with a better blended price of 1.3281 instead of 1.3300 and will still be able to target 1.3400.

3. Buy 100,000 units (now completing 100 percent total position) at 1.3236 (61.8 percent retracement of the candle). Your cost for the trade now declines to 1.3259 from your original entry of 1.3300. If prices simply rally back to your original entry point your trade would already be materially profitable!

4. Put a stop for the whole trade at 1.3220, just below the 76.1 percent Fibonacci level, reasoning that if price has retreated so much, most likely you are wrong on the trade. Furthermore, with such a favorable price average you could shorten your target to 1.3338—the first 138.2 percent Fib projection level—and still enjoy a very attractive 2:1 reward-to-risk ratio on the trade. (Total risk would be 39 points, while potential reward at 1.3338—fully 62 points less than your original target—would be 78 points.

In the second scenario you, the trader, could also afford to lose more than 50 percent of the time and still be profitable on the strategy. Even if you decided to stick to your original target of 1.3400, the lower probability of the trade would be offset by the substantially higher profit gains of the winning trades. At 1.3400 your profit potential would rise to 140 points while your risk remains at 39 points.

Which scenario is best? They both have their drawbacks. In the first example, the trader is vulnerable to a quick reversal if the price just reaches the 161.8 percent target level and then suddenly falls back through the original entry level taking the trader out of the trade and then just as quickly rallying to 1.3400. In that case the trader would be best served if he had simply entered the position all at once at 1.3300 with a hard stop at 1.3280. In the second example the trader is at risk of being underinvested as price moves in his favor right away and overinvested in a losing position if it doesn't.

Ultimately, however, these strategies can help the FX trader to better manage positions by adjusting to market action. As Josh Lukeman contends in his book, professionals understand prices are always fluid and they never make the mistake of committing all their speculative capital to a single price point. By utilizing Fibonacci levels as malleable markers for support and resistance price zones rather than exact price points, technically oriented traders can put Fibonacci levels to practical use, even if the quasi-mystical emphasis on their relevance is somewhat suspect.

CHAPTER 8

Patterns and Antipatterns: Know Your Mark

In the movie *Rounders* the climactic scene takes place between Matt Damon as a young card shark and a menacing Russian mobster called Teddy KGB, played with slouching malevolence by John Malkovich. Damon and Malkovich are playing high-stakes poker in a garishly lit New York private club and Damon is about to call when he sees Malkovich twist open an Oreo cookie and calmly lick out the middle in a casual gesture of self-satisfaction. Damon hesitates and then quickly folds.

Stunned, Malkovich's character blurts out angrily, "No! you were supposed to bet!" Damon of course goes on to win the game, recover all his money, and head to California to reunite with the girl of his dreams and live happily ever after. Why did Damon withdraw his bet at the last moment? Because the exact same dynamic occurred at the beginning of the movie when Teddy KGB devoured the Oreo cookie in the same manner just prior to setting Damon up and winning all of Damon's life savings. This time the Damon character caught the move before falling into Malkovich's trap.

In poker this practice of looking for key patterns of behavior is called "reading a tell," and world-class poker players are masters at not only playing the cards but also observing their opponents' physical moves for any potential clues to the strength of their hands. So, for that matter, are master con men and master magicians. There once was a wonderful *New Yorker* article on Ricky Jay, a virtuoso magician who in recent years has become a solid character actor in movies and television, including HBO's *Wildwood*. Another magician, an expert at his craft, was stunned at how Mr. Jay was able to pull a complex magic trick on him. "He must have marked me," he says of Mr. Jay, meaning that Ricky had carefully observed the man's behavior and then taken advantage of his habits to set up the magic trick.

In every life situation where only imperfect information exists, observation and pattern recognition are critical to successful decision making. Technical analysis is no different. Common price patterns exist and repeat themselves endlessly. In fact, as I once wrote in an article, "For anyone who has ever actually watched price flow on a tick-by-tick basis for months on end, what soon becomes strikingly clear is not the wild randomness of price patterns, but their mundane repetitiveness." Indeed, the common technical formations are all well known and have long ago been classified. This chapter focuses on not only the basic trading patterns that all technicians look for in the FX market, but also their "antipattern" counterparts, because in order to trade patterns successfully, the well-versed technical trader must also understand how these price patterns can fail and often morph into completely different technical setups.

DOUBLE TOPS AND DOUBLE BOTTOMS

No chart pattern is more common in trading than the double bottom or double top. This pattern appears so often that it alone may serve as proof positive that price action is not as wildly random as many academics claim. If you believe, as I do, that at their core price charts simply express trader sentiment, then double tops and double bottoms represent a retesting of temporary price extremes. If prices were truly random, why do they pause so frequently at just those points? To technically oriented traders the explanation lies in the fact that many market participants are keenly aware of these levels and they serve as clear demarcation lines between the bulls and the bears.

Double tops are characterized by their M shape on the price charts, while double bottoms simply flip the pattern and form a W (see Figures 8.1 and 8.2). The classic double bottom pattern forms when prices finally find some support and begin to bounce. At this point traders who were lucky enough to be short and rode the price action all the way down may begin to cover their positions. The shorts will do so because they want to make sure they lock in their substantial profits. As their buying proceeds, pushing prices up, they will encounter selling from the lucky bottom-fishing longs who are looking to flip their positions for quick gains. Additionally, as prices rise all of the trapped longs who got caught in the downdraft may now find themselves at or near their break-even points and may join the selling spree to liquidate their positions at a minimal loss.

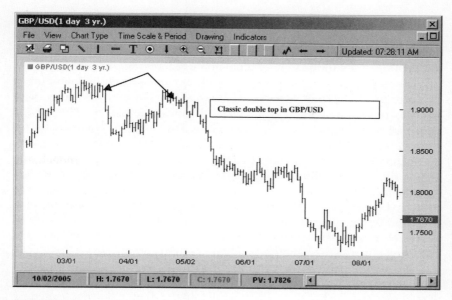

FIGURE 8.1 Double Top in GBP/USD
Source: FXtrek IntelliChart™. Copyright 2001–2005 FXtrek.com, Inc.

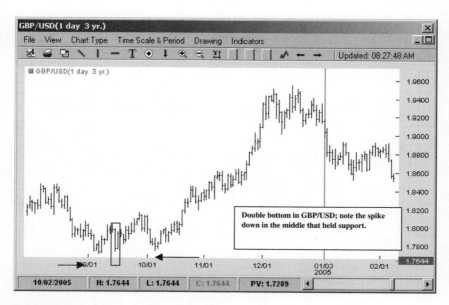

FIGURE 8.2 Double Bottom in GBP/USD
Source: FXtrek IntelliChart™. Copyright 2001–2005 FXtrek.com, Inc.

The net effect of this tug-of-war between the short-covering bears and the liquidating bulls is that the price rarely makes it back up to the original point of its decline. Frequently it may peter out at the 38.2 or 50 or 61.8 Fib levels of the amplitude of the original impulse move (see Figure 8.3).

Prices will then turn back down and may once again find support at the prior low. This time, however, the longs who purchase at these levels typically tend to be longer-term, more value-oriented players who, having observed the initial bottom, will now view it as a solid reference point for support and will likely make a powerful stand at that level. Furthermore, the scared longs who liquidated their positions on the first counterrally up will no longer add selling pressure to the currency, as they are now side-lined in cash. In fact, in watching the price action a few of them may even reenter the market on the long side as they see their initial bias become corroborated by the price action. Buying pressure will also build up from the long-standing shorts, who will realize that directional power has inex-orably returned to the longs and will now want to get out for fear of seeing their winning positions turn into losers. Finally, as prices clear the point from which the decline originated, the last few profitable shorts will capit-ulate and price will break above, completing the double bottom formation (see Figure 8.4).

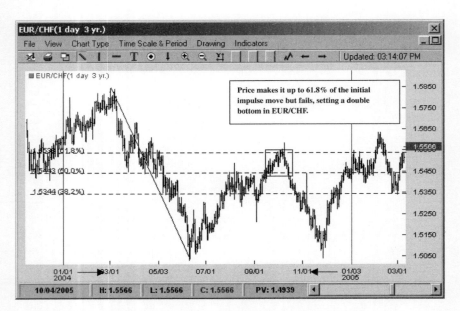

FIGURE 8.3   Double Bottom with Fib Retracement in EUR/CHF
Source: FXtrek IntelliChart™. Copyright 2001–2005 FXtrek.com, Inc.

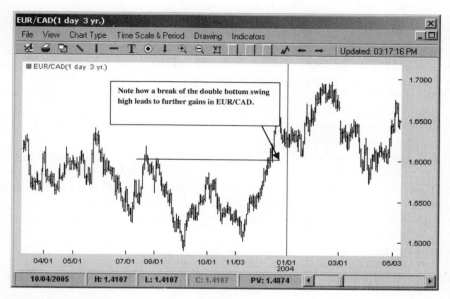

FIGURE 8.4 Double Bottom Breakout in EUR/CAD
Source: FXtrek IntelliChart™. Copyright 2001–2005 FXtrek.com, Inc.

The process of course works the exact same way in reverse for double tops. In that case directional power moves to the bears instead of the bulls as long directional momentum eventually wanes. In both examples it is very clear to see how the interplay between the longer-term, more value oriented players and the shorter-term speculators on both the long side and the short side creates a dynamic that carves out these patterns on a regular basis.

TRIPLE TOPS AND BOTTOMS AND THE ANTIPATTERN

Triple tops and triple bottoms are simply extensions of the double bottom/top price action. Though far rarer, triple tops and bottoms connote uncertainty and a sense of equilibrium between the bulls and the bears as neither party is strong enough to dominate directions. What makes triple tops and bottoms interesting and at the same time dangerous for the technically oriented trader is the possibility that these reversal patterns can morph into consolidation patterns that will provide further fuel for continuation of the trend. This is why traders must be keenly aware of how a double or triple top can turn into a consolidation and a possible further breakout. Note in Figure 8.5 how what initially appeared to be a double bottom slowly turned into range, which eventually broke to the downside as support gave way and the initial downward impulse move resumed its direction.

Because the double top/double bottom pattern that foreshadows a reversal in price can easily turn on the trader and instead become a continuation pattern it is vital to a implement a logical plan of action to deal with all the possible contingencies *before* putting on a trade. There are a variety of approaches to how to trade the double top or bottom, each with its own advantages and drawbacks. Choosing which approach works best is far more a function of trader personality than of the validity of the setup. The critical factor that one must remember is that regardless of which trading style one adopts, the trader must respect the logical assumptions of the scenario and immediately liquidate the position once those assumptions are violated. Traders can be either anticipatory or reactive when trading double tops or double bottoms.

An anticipatory trader would simply assume that the price will find support on the second foray lower and will place his buy order as close as possible to the original bottom and expect that buyers will materialize and will rally the currency pair higher. This is akin to standing in front of an

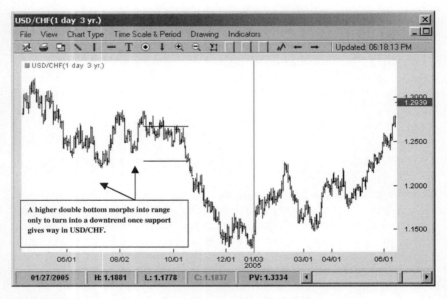

FIGURE 8.5   Double Bottom Becomes Range in USD/CHF
Source: FXtrek IntelliChart™. Copyright 2001–2005 FXtrek.com, Inc.

oncoming train and hoping that the engineer will hit the brakes fast enough for the train to stop before running you over. Needless to say, this is a very low-probability setup. However, when successful this type of trade can be very profitable as the risk-to-reward ratio is very favorable. If the trader is correct, then he has essentially picked the bottom and his first technical level of resistance is the midpoint of the W as seen in Figure 8.6. His next level is the original point of decline. On the daily charts, as we can see in this GBP/USD formation, the move can be as strong as 1,000 points, while the risk is only about 100 points below the first low. With such favorable odds the trader can be wrong as many as nine times in a row and still make a profit over the long run. However, anticipatory traders must be highly disciplined with their stops. Because this type of trade frequently fails, they cannot afford to lose a large amount on any given attempt. The logic behind this setup is that the trader anticipates a bounce. If no bounce materializes, then the trade is no longer valid and for traders who insist on staying in the trade only rationalizations remain.

One of the more frustrating aspects of this approach is that prices will frequently slide below the trader's tight stop only to quickly recover and resume the reversal. Sometimes this process will happen more than once, triggering multiple stops as the anticipatory trader struggles to establish a

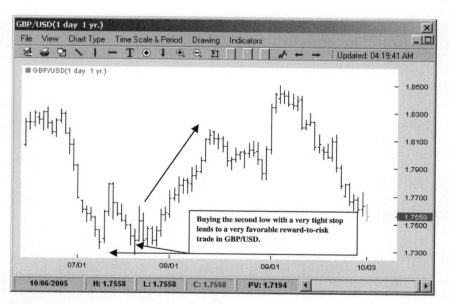

FIGURE 8.6   Double Bottom with Tight Stop
Source: FXtrek IntelliChart™. Copyright 2001–2005 FXtrek.com, Inc.

position. This occurs because many other players in the FX market, including dealers and hedge funds, are perfectly aware of these levels and will gladly go on stop-hunting expeditions to shake out the weaker hands. Nevertheless, traders who decide to relax their stops in response to this price action will pay dearly as it takes only one serious break of support to catch the trader unawares and quickly generate losses of 4, 5, even 10 times his original risk.

Because the anticipatory strategy can be both financially difficult and psychologically draining, some traders prefer the reactive method. Reactive traders, as the name implies, will not "front-run" the price action. Instead they will observe how the price behaves at the key support points in double bottoms and at the key resistance levels in double tops. Only after the price stabilizes at the original lows and then proceeds to make a series of higher lows will the reactive trader enter the trade. Granted, his entry will be inferior to that of the anticipatory trader and his risk-to-reward ratio will not be nearly as favorable, but the probability of success will be higher. Furthermore, the reactive trader will now have a logical reference point in terms of where he should place his stop. Again there are several choices depending on the price action and the temperament of the trader (see Figure 8.7). If price makes a higher double bottom, a trader with low

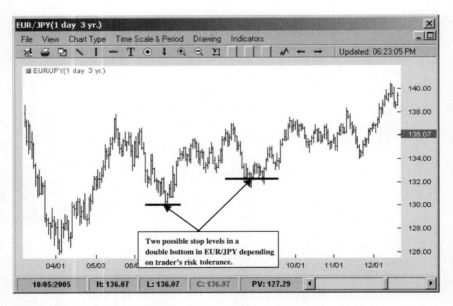

FIGURE 8.7 Double Bottom with Variable Stop
Source: FXtrek IntelliChart™. Copyright 2001–2005 FXtrek.com, Inc.

risk tolerance can use the most recent low as his stop. The risk will be smaller but the possibility of stop-outs is far higher since price can easily trade down to the original low to truly test support. More aggressive traders may therefore choose to set their stops at the original low of the double bottom rather than the most recent low. This in fact is the most logical stop point. If price breaks support, the double bottom has now changed into a consolation range with high probability of continuation lower. The pattern has become the antipattern.

A more unusual version of the double bottom occurs when the second bottom is lower than the first. This type of pattern actually occurs with relative frequency in FX and again shows the subtle power of former support and resistance levels. The "lower low" double bottom and its opposite, the "higher high" double top, simply demonstrate the fact that the dominant directional group had enough momentum to break the original support or smash original resistance but then quickly ran out of gas. This pattern also shows the particular advantages of a reactive approach, which would simply observe the action and act only when support appeared to have been set. The anticipatory trader would of course be stopped out shortly after prices collapsed through the original bottom.

One difficult task for reactive traders is to determine exactly what constitutes support and to know when a second bottom has been put into place. Some traders suggest using a 7 percent retracement rule. The trader would simply measure the full amplitude of the downtrend from its peak to its lowest low, and if price bounced up by 7 percent or greater of the length of the downtrend, the reactive trader would assume that a double bottom had been made at the lowest low. Figure 8.8 shows how that method would work.

The 7 percent rule is of course arbitrary, since it is impossible to determine with great accuracy the exact point of support. One can only speculate and make intelligent assessments of probabilities, which is what trading is really all about. Nevertheless, the 7 percent approach offers the reactive trader a reasonable method for quickly identifying a bottom. Another way to identify the same possibility and one that I personally prefer is to wait for price to make at least three higher periodic lows to confirm that a second bottom has been put in place. That type of entry may position the reactive trader a bit later relative to the turn but it will also provide a more accurate reading of the price flow. Regardless of how one chooses to enter this trade, the clear stop behind this setup is the lowest low of the second bottom. If that low is broken, more selling is likely and the lower double bottom has simply turned into a creeper downtrend. Again, the pattern is now the antipattern, and woe to the trader who refuses to acknowledge that fact. Refer to Figure 8.9 for a view of that dynamic.

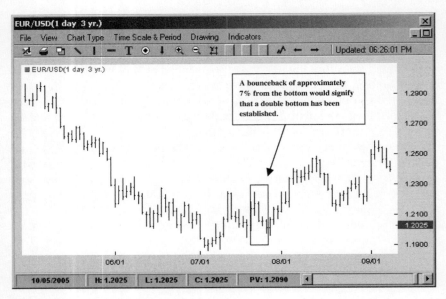

FIGURE 8.8 Seven Percent Bounceback Rule
Source: FXtrek IntelliChart™. Copyright 2001–2005 FXtrek.com, Inc.

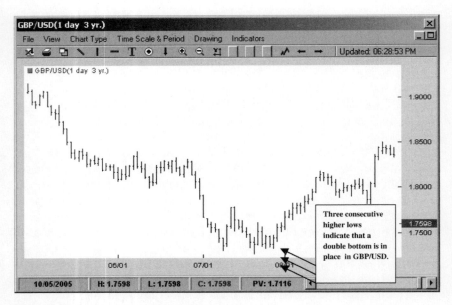

FIGURE 8.9 Three Consecutive Higher Lows
Source: FXtrek IntelliChart™. Copyright 2001–2005 FXtrek.com, Inc.

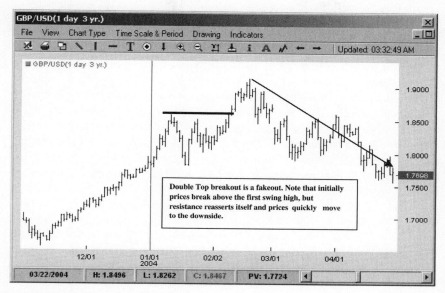

FIGURE 8.10 Double Top Fakeout
Source: FXtrek IntelliChart™. Copyright 2001–2005 FXtrek.com, Inc.

Perhaps the most interesting lesson of the fakeout double bottoms and double tops (the ones that have lower lows and higher highs) is that traders should never quit on possible patterns. Even if prices blow through the initial support or resistance levels they may foreshadow a trade setup in the near future. Just like gravity, these original levels may act as brakes on any forward momentum, and even if they don't stop the price action at the original support or resistance point the turn may occur in the near future (see Figure 8.10). That is why it is critical to follow the price action of the currency closely even if the original point of support or resistance is broken. The true reversal may be near at hand.

FLAGS AND PENNANTS

If double tops and double bottoms are the most popular reversal patterns, then surely bear and bull flags are the most popular continuation patterns. Both of these patterns occur after a sharp directional move and generally connote that price is entering a consolidation stage before pushing higher or lower. The directional move is known as the flagpole and must precede the price action in order for the pattern to be valid. Note the examples of both bull and bear flags in Figure 8.11 and Figure 8.12 with their concomitant extensions.

It is interesting to see flag formations in different contexts. Note for example how in Figure 8.13 when we apply our Bollinger band "bands" the flag is nothing more than a retracement within a channel or in Figure 8.14 it is simply the V of the W bottom. It is quite helpful to break up these patterns into their component pieces to understand how each pattern can transform into another one. Note, for example, that a pattern that begins as a bear flag, then fails to penetrate the bottom of the flagpole and becomes a double bottom, turns in the process from a continuation pattern into a reversal move.

Like the flag, the pennant shares the flagpole, but unlike the flag, which is a small rectangular pattern that slopes against the previous trend, the pennant is comprised of an asymmetrical triangle that opens wide and eventually compresses to a conelike shape. The easiest way to distinguish the two is that in the case of the bear flag the lows of the rectangle will be progressively higher whereas in the case of a bear pennant the lows will be relatively equal, forming the perfect base of the triangle (see Figure 8.15).

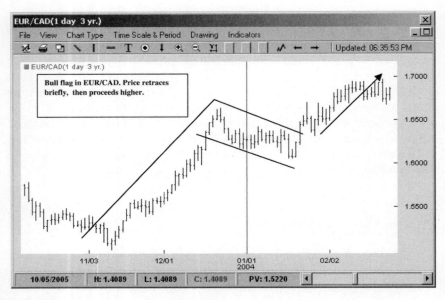

FIGURE 8.11   Bull Flag in EUR/CAD
Source: FXtrek IntelliChart™. Copyright 2001–2005 FXtrek.com, Inc.

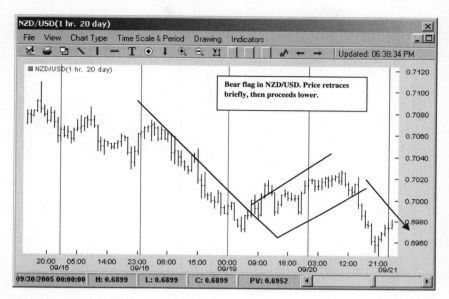

FIGURE 8.12 Bear Flag in NZD/USD
Source: FXtrek IntelliChart™. Copyright 2001–2005 FXtrek.com, Inc.

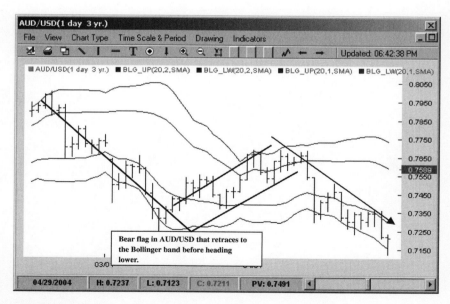

FIGURE 8.13 Bear Flag Retracement to Bollinger Band "Band" in AUD/USD
Source: FXtrek IntelliChart™. Copyright 2001–2005 FXtrek.com, Inc.

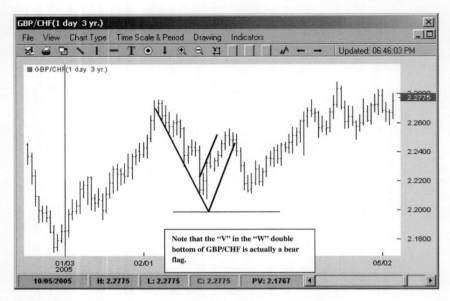

FIGURE 8.14   Bear Flag in the Double Bottom of GBP/CHF
Source: FXtrek IntelliChart™. Copyright 2001–2005 FXtrek.com, Inc.

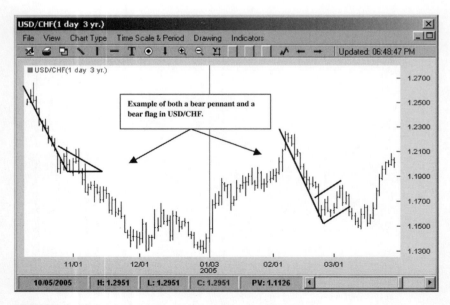

FIGURE 8.15   Bear Pennant and Bear Flag in USD/CHF
Source: FXtrek IntelliChart™. Copyright 2001–2005 FXtrek.com, Inc.

Both patterns are confirmed when their respective flagpole tops or bottoms are penetrated and the price resumes its original direction. Basically flags and pennants demonstrate a pause in market action. Just as we sometimes must sit quietly and digest the main course before we can tackle dessert, so must the market absorb new price levels and test the resolve of both the bulls and the bears before making further moves.

Because of their subtle differences, flags and pennants offer some different setups. While the classic way to trade them is by waiting for the breakout to occur and follow the continuation of price flow, the flag pattern, unlike the more constrained pennant, offers another opportunity for profit. Because the flag produces a much sharper retracement path than the pennant, we can participate in the trade not only at the point of break of the flagpole but also at the moment of flag failure. Here we can use Fibonacci levels to help us gauge the possible extent of the flag formation and its turning point. Figure 8.16 shows how in a bear flag the price retraces up to the 38.2 percent Fibonacci level and then proceeds to pull downward toward the initial downtrend. A trader could enter the setup when price falls below the 38.2 percent zone, indicating that most of the short covering and countertrend strength is gone, and set the stop at the most recent swing high. If the price reaches the bottom of the flagpole, the

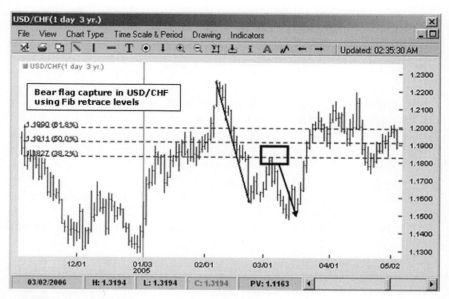

FIGURE 8.16   Bear Flag Capture in USD/CHF
Source: FXtrek IntelliChart™. Copyright 2001–2005 FXtrek.com, Inc.

trader can cover half the position, move the stop to the break-even point, and await the possible break and continuation move.

One of the more attractive aspects of the flag pattern is that it can be traded profitably in this manner even if the pattern eventually fails. Capturing the flag part of the flag pattern can sometimes be as effective as trading the break.

TRIANGLES, WEDGES, AND DIAMONDS

Triangles and wedges are yet another family of consolidation patterns that can offer a variety of profitable setups to the technically oriented trader.

Triangles

There are three key patterns that most technicians focus on:

1. Symmetrical triangle
2. Ascending triangle
3. Descending triangle

The *symmetrical triangle*, which shows price action becoming progressively tighter and compressing like a coil, usually forms during a trend as a continuation pattern. This pattern contains at least two lower highs and two higher lows. When these points are connected on the chart they eventually converge into a fulcrum that typically resolves itself in the direction of the initial trend. That's not always the case, however, and sometimes symmetrical triangles will produce breakdowns in an uptrend and breakouts in a downtrend. Regardless of whether the symmetrical triangle evolves into continuation or reversal, the key to trading it successfully is to wait unit the price action actually makes a move before committing to a setup. Figure 8.17 shows two separate symmetrical triangles with the price resolving in different directions.

Why is this pattern so valuable? Because it perfectly encapsulates the market struggle between the longs and shorts to assert control over price. During the period of consolidation neither the bulls nor the bears can extend their ranges. Thus we have a series of lower highs and higher lows until eventually the price action triangulates and one side blinks. Often in the currency market this pattern can give birth to a powerful move akin to a rubber ball held under water, which when released will thrust upward (see Figure 8.18).

The *ascending triangle* is usually a bullish formation that serves as a

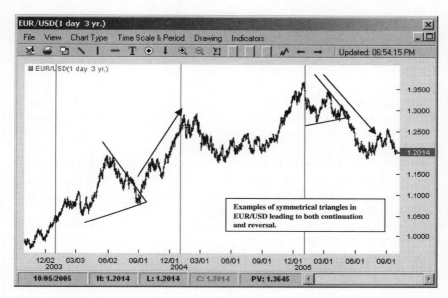

FIGURE 8.17　Symmetrical Triangles in EUR/USD
Source: FXtrek IntelliChart™. Copyright 2001–2005 FXtrek.com, Inc.

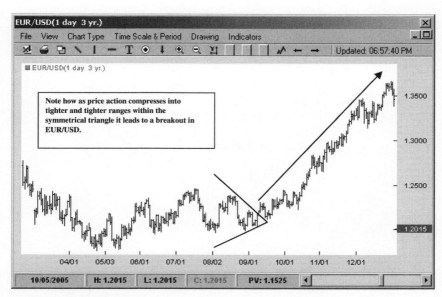

FIGURE 8.18　Symmetrical Triangle Breakout in EUR/USD
Source: FXtrek IntelliChart™. Copyright 2001–2005 FXtrek.com, Inc.

continuation pattern in an uptrend or a reversal pattern in a downtrend. The ascending triangle is distinguished by its series of higher lows and relatively even highs. The higher lows indicate that bulls are accumulating the currency on any and all pullbacks, inexorably building a strong line of support. At the same time the bears provide consistent resistance at the upper level of the range. As time progresses the distance between the two camps inevitably narrows, and typically as the buying pressure from the bulls builds resistance gives way and prices resolve upward (see Figure 8.19).

The general rule of thumb is that the price must make at least three impulse highs and two reaction lows in order for the pattern to qualify as an ascending triangle. In essence, the triangle is composed of series of double tops and higher double bottoms.

Once a breakout is made, the straight line of the ascending triangle that used to serve as resistance now becomes support. Most traders would be wise to place their stops near that point. However, the exact nature of the stop should be carefully considered. The key tenet of technical analysis is that former resistance becomes new support. The corollary to that rule is that price will quite frequently want to test that former support. In the case of the ascending triangle, the bears may make one last stand and try to drive the prices back through the breakout line. Therefore

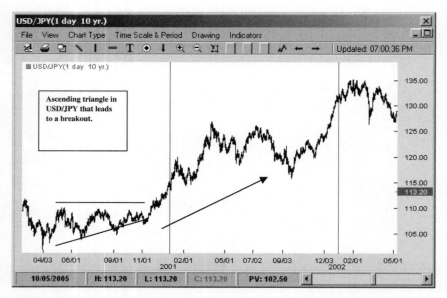

FIGURE 8.19 Ascending Triangle in USD/JPY
Source: FXtrek IntelliChart™. Copyright 2001–2005 FXtrek.com, Inc.

it is important to set stops not at the top line of the triangle, which would risk taking the trader out on a quick burst back to support, but rather at the bottom line of the triangle, which should avoid most of the position-jockeying noise but is still close enough to protect trading capital should the pattern break down and fail (see Figure 8.20).

The *descending triangle* is simply the reverse formation of the ascending triangle. The pattern is bearish and typically forms during a downtrend as a continuation pattern. It can also form as a reversal pattern in an uptrend. The key distinguishing characteristic of the descending triangle is the fact that it is marked by a series of lower and lower highs and relatively equal lows, so that price eventually converges to a point of resolution headed down.

Like the ascending triangle, this pattern requires a minimum of two reaction highs and three reaction lows to be considered valid. The descending triangle basically describes the futile action of the bulls as they stage a series of ever more pathetic rallies, each smaller than the prior one. As the last of the bullish momentum eventually wanes, prices give way and a downward cascade commences.

Whereas the ascending triangle demonstrates accumulation from smart-money bulls who buy every pullback in anticipation of a rally, the descending triangle is a study in distribution where the crafty bears build

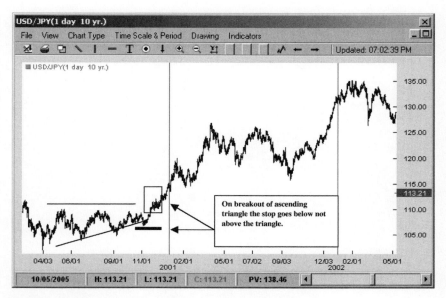

FIGURE 8.20 Placing Stops with Ascending Triangles
Source: FXtrek IntelliChart™. Copyright 2001–2005 FXtrek.com, Inc.

short positions on every rally, confident that prices will eventually crack. Although these patterns can be evident on any time frame, including even the 5-minute charts, they are most powerful when they develop on daily charts over periods of weeks and even months. Prices that form over longer time frames tend to present a much broader array of market consensus. When resolution comes, the moves therefore can be quite powerful. Note in Figure 8.21 how the descending triangle in the GBP/USD on the daily chart ultimately leads to an almost uninterrupted 800-point decline.

Wedges

Wedges can be one of the most difficult patterns to spot because of their subtle, slow formation. The *falling wedge*, for example, is a bullish pattern that connotes a reversal of a downtrend or a continuation of an uptrend. It begins with a wide range and slowly contracts as prices make lower highs and lower lows. The shape of the wedge resembles a cone, although it rarely compresses to a tip. Rather, price ranges continue to narrow until the upper trend line of the wedge is broken to the upside and a rally begins (see Figure 8.22).

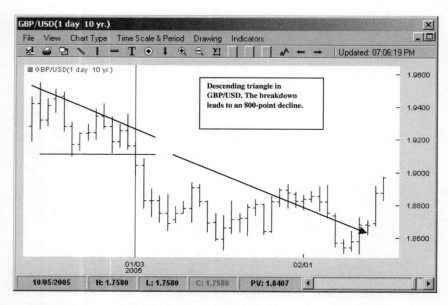

FIGURE 8.21 Descending Triangle in GBP/USD
Source: FXtrek IntelliChart™. Copyright 2001–2005 FXtrek.com, Inc.

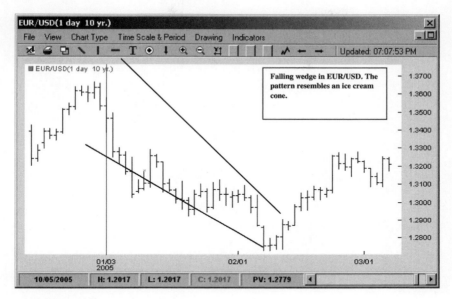

FIGURE 8.22 Falling Wedge in EUR/USD
Source: FXtrek IntelliChart™. Copyright 2001–2005 FXtrek.com, Inc.

The key difference between a symmetrical triangle and a falling wedge is the pronounced nature of the slope of the wedge. The falling wedge will always have a downward-sloping bottom trend line that will connect the series of lower lows. The wedge basically alerts the trader to declining downward momentum and provides clues as to when the move may be exhausted, allowing the trader to position early to take advantage of the turn. As such, using a momentum oscillator like the MACD histogram in conjunction with a falling wedge may be very useful to a trader trying to identify an inflection point (see Figure 8.23).

The *rising wedge*, like its antithesis the falling wedge, is also a long-term pattern, although it is bearish in nature. The rising wedge portrays a slow rise in prices with a series of higher highs and higher lows that provide it with its distinctly upward-leaning slope. Although the rising wedge may appear to be bullish, it is actually telegraphing a warning to a long-biased trader that upward momentum is losing steam as prices coalesce in an ever narrower channel (see Figure 8.24).

The dynamic behind the rising wedge paints a picture where the bulls are able to generate a series of new highs, but each high becomes smaller and smaller. For example, note in Figure 8.25 that GBP/USD first makes a rally 2,000 points in length; then after a retracement the second rally as

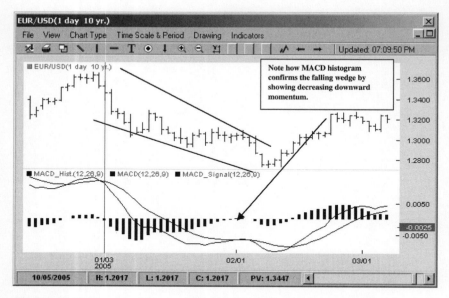

FIGURE 8.23   Falling Wedge Confirmed by MACD Histogram
Source: FXtrek IntelliChart™. Copyright 2001–2005 FXtrek.com, Inc.

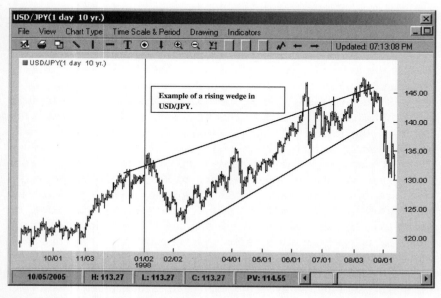

FIGURE 8.24   Rising Wedge in USD/JPY
Source: FXtrek IntelliChart™. Copyright 2001–2005 FXtrek.com, Inc.

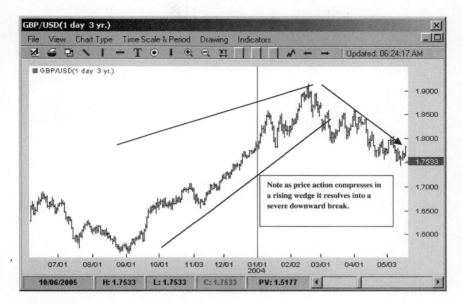

FIGURE 8.25 Rising Wedge Leads to Decline
Source: FXtrek IntelliChart™. Copyright 2001–2005 FXtrek.com, Inc.

measured from its swing bottom to its swing top is only 1,300 points higher; but soon afterward prices give way. In each successive up move prices make new highs but as the length of each move decreases it shows that bulls are becoming less and less productive, much like a bulldozer that can move gravel less and less distance with each successive thrust.

Eventually, as prices make smaller and smaller swing highs, the rising wedge comes to a near halt. If the price retraces, tests the lower end of its channel, and then breaks it, the rising wedge provides a reversal signal that can often lead to a powerful countertrend.

Diamonds

Diamonds are one of the rarest patterns and can be incredibly frustrating for a trader caught within one (see Figure 8.26). The pattern, which is a reversal formation, is found far more frequently at market tops than at bottoms and is consistent with the chaotic, volatile environment that often characterizes such periods. The diamond pattern starts out as a series of higher double or triple tops that consolidates into a symmetrical triangle. This rather bizarre combination of broader price action followed by the narrowing of bars is what gives the diamond its distinctive shape.

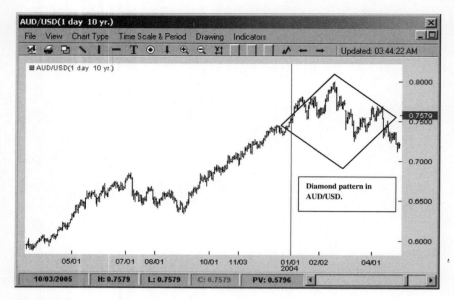

FIGURE 8.26   Diamond Pattern in AUD/USD
Source: FXtrek IntelliChart™. Copyright 2001–2005 FXtrek.com, Inc.

The price action carved by the diamond pattern is the result of wild, wide-ranging swings between the bulls and the bears, which are often a function of emotional short covering and quick, careless stop-outs as both parties become fearful of what may transpire next. Eventually the price action settles into smaller and smaller ranges as both parties, like gunslingers at the O.K. Corral, wait for the other guy to make the next move.

Since the diamonds predominantly occur at the top of the uptrend, the next move is typically down as trend exhaustion sets in and prices fall (see Figure 8.27). The break of the diamond would signal the trade entry point for a technical trader, with the swing top serving as the stop. If prices suddenly reverse and begin to race upward, the diamond will have transformed into a consolidation range, which would be highly indicative of higher prices as bulls have been able to stem the decline. At that point the pattern fails; the trader should recognize that fact and abandon the trade.

Diamond patterns with their high middle spike and winglike structure are quite similar to the final pattern that we'll examine—one that is possibly the best-known price pattern of all: head and shoulders.

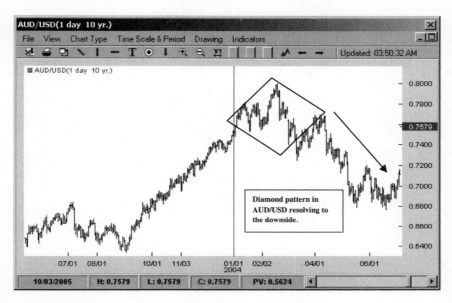

FIGURE 8.27 Diamond Pattern Resolving to Downside
Source: FXtrek IntelliChart™. Copyright 2001–2005 FXtrek.com, Inc.

HEAD AND SHOULDERS

The head and shoulders pattern is one of the most common and famous reversal patterns in all of technical analysis. The formation is basically a very specific type of triple top with the middle peak higher than the two outside peaks. The pattern vaguely resembles a human body; thus the middle peak is known as the head and the two lower peaks are the left and right shoulders. Figure 8.28 shows the classic head and shoulders formation in GBP/USD.

The head and shoulders pattern is formed after a prolonged uptrend in three distinct stages.

1. The left shoulder is created while still in an uptrend as prices rally and then retrace slightly without breaking the upward trend line. This part of the pattern can also be seen as a bull flag.

2. From the low of the left shoulder prices stage a massive rally that takes the currency pair to new highs. Prices then retrace the whole move and find support at or near the low of the left shoulder.

3. Prices again attempt to rally but fail to make new highs. The high of the right shoulder may be greater or smaller than the high of the left

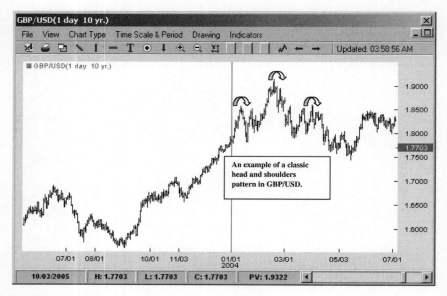

FIGURE 8.28   Head and Shoulders in GBP/USD
Source: FXtrek IntelliChart™. Copyright 2001–2005 FXtrek.com, Inc.

shoulder. However, once again prices fail in their rally, and this time they decline past the bottom set by both the left shoulder and the head. This support line is known as the neckline, and when it breaks the head and shoulders pattern is completed as the full price reversal begins to take place (see Figure 8.29).

REVERSE HEAD AND SHOULDERS

A reverse head and shoulders pattern follows the same dynamic, but simply in the opposite manner with the head making the peak low and the two shoulders completing the reversal pattern to the upside (see Figure 8.30). One of the interesting aspects of both the regular and the reverse head and shoulders pattern is that, just as with all technical patterns, former support becomes resistance and former resistance becomes support. Thus, for example, in the reverse head and shoulders the neckline that initially served as major resistance will now become major support. For traders trading the head and shoulders pattern or its reverse, this line should now serve as a stop point, for if it is violated materially after prices make a breakout, then the pattern is most likely broken and may trans-

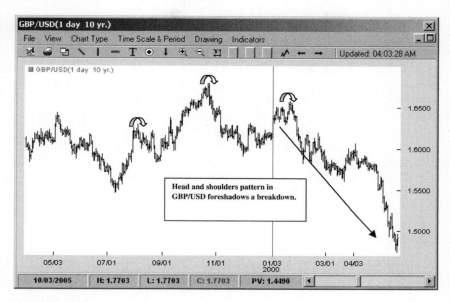

FIGURE 8.29 Breakdown from Head and Shoulders
Source: FXtrek IntelliChart™. Copyright 2001–2005 FXtrek.com, Inc.

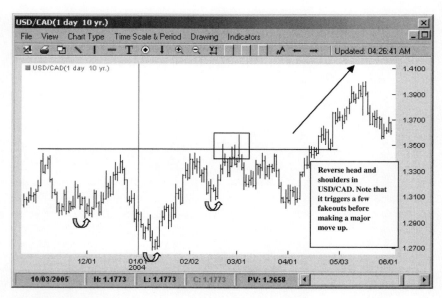

FIGURE 8.30 Reverse Head and Shoulders in USD/CAD
Source: FXtrek IntelliChart™. Copyright 2001–2005 FXtrek.com, Inc.

form into a consolidation range that could eventually see continuation rather than a price reversal.

Setting stops in this case, however, is far more a matter of art than of science. The neckline is a volatile barrier as both bulls and bears make all-out attempts to battle for price dominance. Price may therefore frequently dip below the neckline in the case of the reverse head and shoulders or pierce it in the case of the regular head and shoulders and stop out traders before successfully resuming the pattern.

What is a good strategy for proper stops? There are several possibilities. A trader cam simply set an arbitrary band of 50 or perhaps 100 points below the neckline for the reverse head and shoulders and do the opposite (setting a stop 50 or 100 points above the neckline) for the regular head and shoulders pattern. This strategy may work most of the time, since it should provide ample room to clear most of the market noise from the position. However, another more technically based approach may be more logical and effective: Instead of using a money stop, a technically oriented trader may consider using the low of the first bar that broke through the neckline. Figure 8.31 shows the proper stop. Alternatively for less-aggressive traders the stop could be placed below the low two bars back from the breakout.

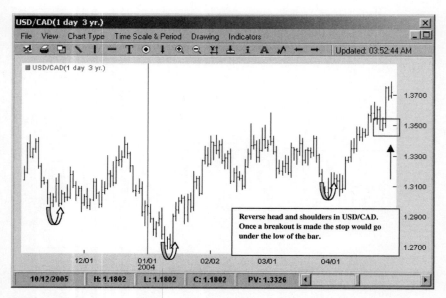

FIGURE 8.31   Proper Stop for Reverse Head and Shoulders
Source: FXtrek IntelliChart™. Copyright 2001–2005 FXtrek.com, Inc.

This approach may be more technically correct, as it uses organic levels generated by the market to provide the trader with reasonable risk parameters. The idea behind using the most recent lows prior to breakout as the stop-out points centers on the fact that they represent the value areas from which the bulls started their rally to complete the reverse head and shoulders pattern. Once those barriers are broken, the probability that the pattern is no longer operable increases significantly.

CONCLUSION

Of course no stops are perfect. It is quite possible to have the price pierce these stops only to violently rally back and resume the reversal. But technical analysis is the study of probabilities, not certainties. Patterns help the trader identify and classify the common behavior traits of market participants. Can this behavior change rapidly? Absolutely—especially in the FX market, which is so heavily driven by economic and geopolitical news that can reverse trader sentiment in a heartbeat.

However, over a long period of time these patterns repeat themselves with almost monotonous regularity. Just as most human behavior is quite predictable over a long period of time, price patterns reflect this psychological dynamic numerous times on the charts. Simply familiarizing yourself with these patterns will not make you profitable. True skill requires experience and solid systematic interpretation of both the price action and the indicator data. Nevertheless, these patterns are the basic building blocks for understanding and interpreting price flow. Just as the greatest literary talent cannot function without the knowledge of the alphabet, so, too, a technically oriented trader cannot be successful without a thorough understanding of how these patterns work.

CHAPTER 9

Know Yourself, Know Your Setup

W ho are you? What are your strengths and what are your weaknesses? Do you thrive amidst chaos or require regimentation and stability? In trading, the answers to these questions are far more important than any setup you can devise. At its core, trading is a game of psychology, and no amount of reading, no computerized back-testing, no advanced seminar work will produce long-term success if your trading style is in conflict with your basic personality. Contrary to popular belief, successful traders do not change their approaches to adjust to the market but rather find market environments that best suit their inherent strengths. That's why in books like Jack D. Schwager's *Market Wizards* (New York Institute of Finance, 1989; HarperBusiness, 1993) you will find very successful traders following diametrically opposite approaches to the market and often dispensing what appears to be contradictory advice. In fact, it's not at all inconceivable to imagine two market wizards taking opposite sides of the same trade yet both walking away with a profit.

To market novices this idea may seem completely illogical. In most businesses we are taught that there is always an optimal way of doing things, that certain processes will be far superior to others. Clearly that's the case with engineering, where scientific rules of optimization and refinement apply to everything from car production to bridge building. Financial markets, however, are emotional mechanisms, which is why engineering-based solutions to trading inevitably fail.

Financial markets are extraordinarily complex with a multitude of players, each with a different agenda and time perspective, providing the trader with a variety of opportunities for profit. Since the currency market is the largest financial market of all, the flexibility to craft a strategy conducive to your specific personality is even better in FX than in any other market. The cold hard truth of life is that we do not really change; we just grow older. The most successful businesspeople in the world learn how to utilize their strengths while minimizing their weaknesses by having their more skilled colleagues perform those tasks which they cannot do well. Trading is very much the same. Successful traders choose those strategies that are most aligned with their psychological profiles while staying out of the market when conditions aren't suitable for their style. It isn't a matter of doing the easy thing or the difficult thing. All trading is difficult. Rather it's a matter of doing the natural thing. Why is this concept so important? Couldn't you simply learn proper trading habits with enough practice and discipline? No. No matter how much discipline you possess, if you are trading contrary to your natural impulses you will eventually sabotage your trading plan and you will fail.

This is the reason why cookie-cutter trading maxims such as "Cut your losses short and let your profits run" are not only useless but often highly destructive for most traders. Each person is unique, and successful currency trading is the art of applying each trader's personal skills to the array of opportunities present in the market.

Let's take a quiz. It is by no means a scientific test. It's just seven simple questions that I devised a while back to help discover potential trading profiles. Don't worry—there are no right or wrong answers. But maybe you will gain some insight into who you are as a trader.

Answer the questions as honestly as possible.

There are no "correct" answers.

You fail only if you lie.

1. You need to buy one important item in the store. You run in quickly, pick it up, and approach the counter. Unfortunately, instead of the usual five cashiers only one cashier is open and there is a line of 20 customers ahead of you. You:

    A. Walk out of the store immediately, leaving your item behind.

    B. Get in line and wait your turn.

2. You are driving down a two-lane highway on your way to work. Suddenly a sports car tries to cut you off, nearly clipping your fender. You:

    A. Slam your horn for at least 15 seconds and wish the driver dead.

    B. Hit the brakes and let the driver pass unimpeded.

3. Assume you are capable of doing both activities. What's more fun?

    A. Fishing.

    B. Downhill skiing.

4. The Powerball lottery jackpot is $100 million. You are at a newsstand buying a magazine when you discover a crumpled $20 bill in a shirt pocket. You:

   A. Buy 20 lottery tickets.

   B. Put the $20 in your wallet.

5. Your favorite entertainer is in town for a surprise show. Your choices are:

   A. Get up at 4 A.M. on Saturday morning to get tickets at the box office.

   B. Buy tickets online for a show nine months later.

6. What is worse:

   A. A constant low-grade toothache for a month?

   B. Having your wisdom tooth pulled with no anesthetic?

7. For the next 52 weeks choose one:

   A. You will be paid $2,000 per week.

   B. You will be paid $700 per week with a reasonable chance but no guarantee to collect a $250,000 bonus.

There is no final score for this test. There are no neat boxes to classify the answers. Rather, they are meant to uncover some inner drives to your behavior that may offer you better clues to what type of trading suits you best.

Let's examine each question in detail.

1. *You need to buy one important item in the store. You run in quickly, pick it up, and approach the counter. Unfortunately, instead of the usual five cashiers only one cashier is open and there is a line of 20 customers ahead of you. You:*

   A. Walk out of the store immediately, leaving your item behind.

   B. Get in line and wait your turn.

How many of us have been in this situation and wanted to scream in frustration? Yet while this question seemingly examines the common problem of modern life, it is actually trying to probe your ability to abandon positions quickly. Will you cut and run at the first sign of trouble or stubbornly wait it out? In other words, answer A says you are likely to take a quick stop-out. Answer B indicates you will nurse a trade, no matter the discomfort.

2. *You are driving down a two-lane highway on your way to work. Suddenly a sports car tries to cut you off, nearly clipping your fender. You:*

   A. Slam your horn for at least 15 seconds and wish the driver dead.

   B. Hit the brakes and let the driver pass unimpeded.

This question tries to ascertain your ability to react to surprising and uncontrollable situations in the market. Do you stoically accept the fate that is dealt you or do you fume in furor over the injustice over it all? Put simply—can you take stops well?

Again, this is not a moral question, but rather one of style. If surprises really unnerve you, the solution is not to learn to repress your emotions but, as we'll see later in the chapter, to apportion your capital in such a way as to avoid a death spiral of impulsive, reckless trading caused by loss of control.

3. *Assume you are capable of doing both activities. What's more fun?*

   A. Fishing.

   B. Downhill skiing.

Surprisingly enough, this is a question about trend and countertrend trading. Fishermen trend, skiers fade. Before I receive letters of protest from trend-following skiers and fading fishermen, allow me to explain. Fishing requires time, methodology, and, most importantly, patience. Fishermen, like trend traders, will cast their line many times before they get a bite. Downhill skiers, on the other hand, look for a quick thrill with a very specific goal—end of run. This psychological drive is similar to that of faders who seek quick profits as currency prices make a quick retracement. Does fishing always lead to trend trading and skiing to countertrend trading? Of course not. However, the activity you choose suggests a definite predilection for one style versus the other.

4. *The Powerball lottery is $100 million. You are at a newsstand buying a magazine when you discover a crumpled $20 bill in a shirt pocket. You:*

   A. Buy 20 lottery tickets.

   B. Put the $20 in your wallet.

This question is really a measure of a trader's preference to trade long shots. If you are willing to bet the lotto, that means you are willing to take a very low-probability trade. Again that fact in and of itself is not necessarily detrimental to a trader's success. As we will see later, if done properly currency speculation allows the trader to place highly improbable bets while limiting overall risk. However, if you chose A, you need to understand that you will most likely lose. A very common problem among traders is the tendency to trade long shots with the expectation to win frequently. This inability to reconcile action with expectation probably leads to more trader failure than all other problems.

5. *Your favorite entertainer is in town for a surprise show. Your choices are:*

   A. Get up at 4 A.M. on Saturday morning to get tickets at the box office.

   B. Buy tickets online for a show nine months later.

This is a question of trading goals. Do you seek immediate gratification and are willing to pay the price to get it? Are you willing to stare at the screen 18 to 20 hours 5 days per week and then scrupulously review every single trade over the weekend? Then you most likely picked A. Or are you more long term oriented? Are you willing to delay your desire for quick cash in order to live a less-demanding lifestyle? Then B is your choice. Note if you picked B but have the goals of a trader who picked A, you are unlikely to realize them.

6. *What is worse:*

   A. A constant low-grade toothache for a month?

   B. Having your wisdom tooth pulled with no anesthetic?

Since neither choice is at all pleasant, this of course is a question about stop-losses. The issue that this question tries to determine is this: Are you more comfortable taking a long series of small losses or would you rather take an occasional large loss? How one honestly answers this question is crucial in determining what style to trade.

7. *For the next 52 weeks choose one:*

   A. You will be paid $2,000 per week.

   B. You will be paid $700 per week with a reasonable chance but no guarantee to collect a $250,000 bonus.

No doubt entrepreneurially minded, free-market-loving traders would scoff at the idea of a steady paycheck and will inevitably choose B. But check your ego at the door and ask yourself, are you really comfortable with this type of volatility? In choice A you stand to make $104,000 per year. In choice B you make either $286,400 or only $36,400 per year. In other words, you can almost triple your salary of choice A or make only about one-third as much. If this disparity truly doesn't bother you and you therefore chose B, then a highly aggressive, high-leverage strategy may be more your style. However, if wide disparity in outcome does bother you, that type of trading will be financial suicide. Instead a totally different approach must be pursued.

Let's examine in detail some strategies that may be of use depending on what type of trader you are. Just as in trading there are really only two decisions to make—trend or fade—so, too, in money management there are only two strategies to follow: You can either suffer numerous small losses and hope that an occasional large win will more than offset the drawdowns in your account or you can harvest many small profits and suffer an occasional large loss that you hope doesn't overwhelm the profit cushion you have built. Of course novice traders rarely face these two choices. They simply lose money. Some lose money in small increments over a long period of time, while others lose money in shockingly huge chunks and are out of the game before they even have a chance to learn how to properly use their trading software. Why do novices inevitably lose? Because they trade in a random fashion. They rarely practice consistency in their setups. They rarely understand the dynamics of price flow, and even when they learn it, they frequently misunderstand the nature of technical analysis.

A while back I received an e-mail from a very nice and earnest former student. He wrote:

Boris—

I was always taught and was repeatedly told that when it comes to a break of support or resistance, the confirmation of such a break is a clean break followed by price exceeding the close of the breaking candle.

The 61.8 percent Fib of the June and July bullwave for EUR/CHF came in at 1.5434, cleanly broken on September 1st when price closed at 1.5412. The next day the price fell further, closing at 1.5399 and inducing me to take a large short.

Having seen this proved false several times (although never as starkly as this or as expensively), I am of the firm opinion that we can take the above philosophy and consign it to the trash for the myth that it is. Would I not at least be right to take it extremely lightly as yet another one of those theories that has more than a 50 percent exception rate?

To which I replied:

This is actually a perfect example of how technical analysis is in the eye of the beholder. First and foremost, there never ever was such a concept as "always" in technical analysis, only "likely." We are forever dealing in probabilities here.

Second, why did this trade work out badly for you? Looking at the chart, I see the first natural stop at 1.5486, above the high of the breakdown candle on September 1. It hasn't even come close to breaking it yet.

I actually really like EUR/CHF short as I think the Swiss will outperform the EU in the near term. Having said that, I hate trading breakout and breakdown because I always feel like I am chasing price flow, but that is my personal prejudice.

One idea you might consider is to wait a bit and try to short the retracement—in this case maybe at 1.5430. You risk the chance of losing out on the trade but gain a better entry, which will make your risk/reward more favorable.

Note, by the way, that this trade turned out to be a loser, regardless of how you traded it. EUR/CHF raced higher, stopping out all approaches to short it. But that's not the point here. The key to understanding the problem is that this trade was only a probability, not a guarantee. Furthermore, by using technical analysis we set logical risk parameters for the trade and, although we took a loss, it was good trade because we reacted properly to market conditions.

Trading randomly, however, is one of the quickest ways to lose money in FX. Many threads on many Internet bulletin boards have been started using the random entry "coin flip" approach and some basic form of money management like risking $1 for every $2 of profit; within a matter of weeks or months, the originators of those threads have found themselves either in deep drawdown or completely broke. Ironically enough, the practitioners of the random entry method inadvertently prove that market action is not random. If it were random, then they presumably should perform no worse than skilled traders; but alas, like a lucky idiot who sinks a half-court shot during a contest but could never win a one-on-one game against a professional basketball player, so, too, these novice traders will fall by the wayside when competing against professional technical traders over any reasonable length of time.

So the notion that technical analysis doesn't matter—it's just money management that matters—is, like so many trading myths, complete nonsense. Money management alone will not make you a successful trader. It is, however, a vital complement to any intelligent technical setup. Furthermore, money management strategies are as unique as each trader, and one of the most pernicious myths perpetrated on the gullible public is that money management strategies are sacrosanct and inviolable and thus all traders must follow the same money management rules in order to achieve success. That is utter nonsense. In fact, the longer the traders trade, the more flexible, the more complex, the more creative their money management skills become. Because FX offers retail traders unprecedented liquidity and limitless customization, money management strategies in FX are truly variable.

THE MYTH OF 2:1

Let's start the most classic money management technique preached by every trading book ever printed. In every trade your reward/risk ratio must be at least 2 to 1. You must try to obtain 2 points of gains for 1 point of risk. This way the trader needs be correct only 40 percent of the time and will still have a positive expectancy to his trades. On the surface this idea sounds eminently logical and practical. In real life consider what this means, however. It's quite difficult to squeeze out 2 points of profit for 1 point of risk. Try it and see. First look at the price action on the smallest time frame and see how hard it is to risk 1 point in order to capture 2 points. On the smallest level the FX trader faces the overwhelming barriers of the spread. Even in the most liquid financial instrument in the world, the EUR/USD, the spread is 3 points wide, so in effect the trader must make 5 points in order to earn 2, thus forcing him to generate an improbable ratio of 5:1 in order to simply meet this goal. Moving on to a 10-point increment, a 10-point risk for a 20-point profit still requires a 23-point gain and allows for only a 7-point risk of loss in the tightest spread pairs like EUR/USD and USD/JPY; in effect, this means that a trader must generate 3 points of profit for 1 point of risk just to meet the 2:1 reward/risk ratio. Expanding the time line to longer time frames, a 100-point risk with a 200-point profit target provides much better odds. Here the spread plays a minuscule part as it requires only 203 points of profit and allows for 97 points of risk, generating very close to a 2:1 ratio.

But let's step back a second. Remember the quiz? What if you were the downhill racer? What if you were the customer who left the long line at the drugstore? In short, what if you were simply not predisposed to patiently stay in the trade for the time necessary to see it to fruition? If you were impatient, wouldn't it be much more probable that you would try to take your profits far sooner, perhaps at 100 points in the money or even 50 points in the money, turning what in effect was supposed to be a 2:1 trade into a 1:1

or 1:2 reward-to-risk setup? You will do what every trading book preaches not to—you will cut your profits short by not letting them run. But given your personality, can you really be expected to do it any differently?

But let's suppose that you are different. You possess the patience of a saint, you have the discipline to follow this rule inviolably. Imagine the following scenario: You place a trade in EUR/USD. Let's say you decide to short the pair at 1.2500 with a 1.2600 stop and a target of 1.2300. The trade is going well. The price moves your way. EUR/USD first drops to 1.2400, then to 1.2350, and slowly makes its way toward 1.2300. At 1.2335 the price action pauses and the pair starts to inch back up, first trading through 1.2350, then 1.2375. You, however, are patient. You have nerves of steel. You hold on, looking for your 2:1 reward-to-risk. The price starts to move back down and you are starting to feel vindicated. Back to 1.2350, 1.2325; slowly but surely you see the target in sight. 1.2320, 1.2310, 1.2305. Your take-profit order sits on the platform waiting to be filled. The price ticks a few more pips down, reaching all the way to 1.2301—but then it bounces back, first slightly, then violently, until in a matter of seconds it's at 1.2350, then 1,2370. You remain calm. The price nearly touched your target. It's bound to test that level again. You won't make the same mistake others make of cutting your profits short. You will stay in the trade and follow the classic money management rules!

Of course, the price never does see 1.2300. Instead the pair verticalizes and soon reaches 1.2600, easily taking out your stop. You are now faced with the idea that you had a 199-point profit and allowed it to become a 100-point loss. Welcome to real trading. How many episodes like that do you think a novice trader can experience before abandoning all sense of discipline and proper money management? This is the reason why the 2:1 reward-to-risk strategy is mostly a fantasy, an ideal. In practice most traders will modify the strategy in one of two ways. First and foremost, once price moves in the direction of the trade by the amount of points risked, professional traders will move their stop-loss to the breakeven point to assure themselves that a winning trade will not become a losing trade. So in the case of our EUR/USD trade the trader would move the stop to 1.2500 once the price breached the 1.2400 level. This, however, still presents a dilemma for most traders. Suppose the price decided to retrace and came all the way back to 1.2500, stopping the trader out. There would be no losses, but also no gains. The trade would be a scratch. In trading there is nothing more frustrating and psychologically unnerving than to be right on direction and walk away with no profit. It's the equivalent of working very hard all day long at your job and then losing that day's pay through a hole in your pocket.

For this reason many traders practice a scale-out approach. Typically traders will let go of half of their position once the gains match their risk value. In our tried-and-true EUR/USD example the trader would sell half at 1.2400 and then move the stop to the break-even point, assuring himself of harvesting at least some profit out of the trade. This approach allows the trader to remain in the trade for as long as necessary because it satisfies the most basic desire of trading—the need to get paid. By selling half of the position at 1.2400 and half at 1.2300, the trader is able to harvest only a 1.5:1 reward-to-risk ratio, which of course is mathematically inferior to 2:1. However, trading is not a game of mathematics but one of psychology, and frequently what is mathematically optimal is psychologically disastrous.

Professional traders recognize this fact well. They also understand than market dynamics are fluid and will rarely conform to rigid reward/risk ratios. By constantly monitoring their positions and adjusting their risk parameters to the reality of the markets, professional traders are able to not only generate positive reward/risk ratios but also produce more profitable trades.

KILLER INSTINCT

Do you have the killer instinct? Can you press the trade? Then this trade management technique may be for you. If you ever want to hit home runs, if you ever want to make a huge score in trading, then this is the only way for you to trade and FX is the single best market to effect this strategy.

Let's take our EUR/USD trade. Again you, the trader, get short at 1.2500 but this time your strategy is different. If the pair trades up to 1.2550, you cut your loss quickly and await the next opportunity. If, however, the trade moves your way, you do not automatically take half the position out of the market. Rather you wait patiently and watch the price action. Imagine the price has now moved to 1.2200, fully 300 points in the money. Instead of taking profits, you add another unit to the trade. If the price begins to retrace all the way back to 1.2350, you cover the whole position for a scratch. You haven't lost anything on the trade, but neither have you made a profit. If, however, the price retraces only slightly but then resumes direction, you stay in position and again monitor price action carefully. The price has now reached 1.2000 and you sell yet one more unit at that price. You now have sold three units altogether for an average price of 1.2230. As long as the price remains below this level, you stay in the trade. Your patience pays off and the price collapses to 1.1700, at which point you finally cover the whole position. Let's review the total profits from the trade:

1 unit at 1.2500 covered at 1.1700 results in a profit of +800 points.

1 unit at 1.2200 covered at 1.1700: +500 points.

1 unit at 1.2000 covered at 1.1700: +300 points.

Total profit: 1,500 points.

Total risk: 50 points.

For those traders who can implement this strategy, this is clearly the best way to trade. Dennis Gartman (the famous investment newsletter writer), an old pit trader himself, calls this method "doing more of what is working and less of what is not." It is no doubt deceptively simple and seductive. In fact, here is a description taken from Elite Trader bulletin board of another famous pit trader, Richard Dennis, employing just such a strategy in the bonds.

> *As someone who has seen the likes of Rich Dennis and Tudor Jones operate, those "5%" winning trades involve add-on after add-on. Case in point is Dennis in the 1985–1986 bull market in bond futures. He would start with his normal unit of 500 contracts and get chopped for days. Buy the day's high, put 'em back out on a new swing low etc. Every once in a while he'd wind up with 500 that worked. Then he'd start the process higher, all over again. Work 'em in, work 'em out. After maybe a couple of months the market has rallied 10 pts. from where he started and he has 2,000 on (meaning 2 million a point). Now the market is short and ready to pop on any size buying and he's there supplying the noose. Bidding for 500 on every uptick, he finally gets to a point where for the last month of the move he has 5,000 on. T-bonds rally 20 pts. in just over a month and he's up $100,000,000 on a trade that started out with him just testing the waters, losing $100,000 a few times before he could establish a position worth doubling up on.*

Wouldn't we all want to own that trade? One trade, $100 million in profit. But let's remember what's required to get there.

- Accurate directional entry into trend.
- An intense, multi-hundred-point trend with little or virtually no retracement along the way.

What are the chances that this type of strategy succeeds? Minimal at best. Note that the writer described these as "5%" trades, meaning that they occurred only 5 percent of the time. In fact, the perfect confluence of events to generate such profits probably happens less than that.

Far more than the fortuitous market conditions necessary to produce such windfall profits is the unbelievable psychological pressure such trading will generate. The term "pressing the trade" is most apropos to describe this dynamic. Not only is the trader pressing the market by adding more and more units as they go deep into the money, but he is also pressed by the market as his profits pile up. Put yourself in Richard Dennis's place. Would you be able to stay in the trade once it hit $1 million? How about $10 million? $50 million? At each level the intensity is enormous, and for most people the pressure of winning can be far worse than the fear of losing. Forget Richard Dennis and just think how you would have felt if after selling the third unit at 1.2000 you had to cover at 1.2233 as prices retraced, and you had to watch a certain profit of 700 points evaporate into nothingness.

For those unconcerned with such issues, for traders who are more than willing to suffer a long series of losses and empty trades for a chance to score big, FX offers the best opportunity to do so of any financial market in the world. Why? Leverage and liquidity.

Here is how this strategy would work. Assume that you have $10,000 of trading capital.

Deposit only $2,000 of capital with your FX dealer. Keep the rest in your bank account. With 100:1 leverage, which is standard in the FX market, you will have 100 points of leeway before you get a margin call in EUR/USD. (Trading other pairs the margin requirements might be different, so consult with your dealer before attempting this idea on other currencies.) If the trade moves against you, an automatic margin call will instantly take you out of the market. Dealers will not call you in advance and warn you of an impending margin call like they may do in exchange-based futures markets. Rather, the dealer's software program will automatically liquidate your position. This may seem a bit brusque, but the upside of such an arrangement is that your account should never experience negative equity and your total risk should be limited to the amount you've deposited. The margin call will then act as a de facto stop on your account.

If a margin call is triggered, your account should have approximately $1,000 of equity left.

$2,000 initial deposit – $1,000 loss on trade
($10 × 100 points at 100:1 leverage) = $1,000

Deposit another $1,000 from your bank and trade again once your setup is triggered. You can repeat this process up to nine times before you run out of your trading capital. Will you lose most of your money? Perhaps. Remember, this is a very low-probability trade. But at least by subdividing your capital into 10 equal pieces you've given yourself the best opportunity to succeed. This strategy is basically a more intelligent variation on the old trader saying, "Have a hunch, bet a bunch."

Let's imagine, however, that on one of the trades you were successful and caught the large directional move. If that's the case, you could employ the trade management strategy discussed before and continuously add to your position as prices move your way. In the best of all possible scenarios the trader could eventually build up a large position, perhaps 10 lots or more (with notional value of $1 million), that could be 1,000 points in the money. In that case the profit on the trade would grow to $100,000. Not bad for $1,000 of initial risk.

As I've already noted, this strategy is not for the faint of heart. This is a very high-risk, (potential) high-reward strategy that requires a unique mindset and proper trade management techniques to succeed. Fortunately, FX is perhaps the single best market to put these ideas into practice.

For those inclined toward a more steady approach, here is a completely different trade methodology and one that I employ myself.

TAKE A NIBBLE, NOT A BITE

Never add to a loser.

Never double down.

These old trading maxims are treated as sacrosanct truths by most traders.

What a bunch of nonsense. I add to losers all the time, and so do some of the most successful traders I know. Why? Because what most books never tell you is that almost all trades start out as losers. It is extremely difficult to time the entry so well that it immediately begins to move in the direction of your trade. Sometimes trades will move only a few points against the position but occasionally prices may retrace several hundred points away from initial entry only to eventually turn around and become profitable. Trading is the art of accurately forecasting direction and timing. Between the two, timing is far harder to handicap, especially if prices seesaw back and forth for a while before ultimately moving in the right direction. Traders who trade highly leveraged positions with tight stops will be eviscerated in such an environment, as they will continuously get stopped out. Far worse than even the hit to equity is the psychological pain of "death by a thousand stops."

That is why traders who do not like frequent stop-outs prefer the scale-in approach to price entry. This strategy is almost diametrically opposite to the strategy discussed in the preceding section. Using the scale-in approach assumes that the first entry will almost never be the best entry; as a result, the approach requires very low leverage in order for the strategy to withstand the adverse price moves. In this strategy the trader continuously adds more units as prices move against him, trying to achieve a blended price that remains near the current price. If prices do eventually turn, the constant averaging of price levels will make the position profitable much faster than if he expended all of his trading capital on the first price entry. While this can be a successful trading strategy, it can also be highly dangerous if the trader does not follow two key rules:

1. Set a hard stop for the whole position.
2. Trade in very small increments.

To understand just how destructive this strategy can be, let's examine what happens if the trader uses this method employing the standard allocation of 2 percent of capital per trade. Imagine that the trader with a trading account of $10,000 initiates the first trade in the EUR/USD currency using two mini lots. Prices move against his entry by 100 points and he now doubles his allocation to four mini lots. Again prices continue to move against him by another 100 points and he doubles his position yet again to eight mini lots. Prices continue to follow this adverse pattern and move against him by 100 points more. Finally, the trader gives up and covers his position in dismay. What is his total loss? A whopping 22 percent of his total capital!

–$600 on two mini lots (prices moved 300 points away from entry).

–$800 on four mini lots (prices moved 200 points away from entry).

–$800 on eight mini lots (prices moved 100 points away from entry).

The irony of the matter is that after an uninterrupted 300-point move against the position, chances are quite high that the trade may turn around and could quickly become profitable. But by overleveraging the position the trader is unable to withstand the drawdown.

Imagine the same scenario but instead of using mini lots with the value of $1 per point, the trader uses micro lots with each point having a value of only 1 dime. In FX, where many dealers offer such small lot sizes, this strategy is eminently possible. In that case the drawdown would be a far more manageable 2.2 percent of capital and the price would need to move back only 150 points instead of the full 300 points in order for the trade to become profitable.

This type of scaling where the trader doubles the size of the position at every interval is called geometric scaling. Unlike regular average-in scaling that cuts the break-even point by 50 percent, geometric scaling requires that prices retrace by only 33 percent to reach the break-even point. While this can be a very effective way to quickly make a losing trade

TABLE 9.1 Geometric versus Arithmetic Scaling

		Arithmetic	Notional Value	Geometric	Notional Value
Long Every 50 Pips Down	1.2500	100	$ 125	100	$ 125
	1.2450	200	$ 249	200	$ 249
Starting Account $5,000	1.2400	300	$ 372	400	$ 496
Unit = 100	1.2350	400	$ 494	800	$ 988
Pip Value = 1 Cent	1.2300	500	$ 615	1,600	$ 1,968
	1.2250	600	$ 735	3,200	$ 3,920
	1.2200	700	$ 854	6,400	$ 7,808
	1.2150	800	$ 972	12,800	$ 15,552
	1.2100	900	$1,089	25,600	$ 30,976
	1.2050	1,000	$1,205	51,200	$ 61,696
	1.2000	1,100	$1,320	102,400	$122,880
		6,600	$8,030	204,700	$246,658
Hard Stop	1.1950				
Break-Even Value		1.2166			1.2049
Maximum Loss in Pips		−143			−2,041.5
Maximum Loss in Dollars		−143			−2,041.5

profitable, the strategy can also spiral out of control. A better compromise between the straight average-in method and the geometric scale-in is the arithmetic scale strategy. Instead of doubling up the position at every interval, the arithmetic scale calls for an increase of the position by a fixed amount. Table 9.1 shows the key differences between the geometric and arithmetic approaches using a hypothetical scale-in strategy in EUR/USD starting with entry at 1.2500 and a hard stop at 1.1950.

Note that in the worst-case scenario the geometric strategy loses more than $2,000 on a $5,000 account while the arithmetic strategy loses only $143. At the same time the break-even point on the arithmetic strategy is 1.2166, only slightly higher than the 1.2049 break-even on the geometric approach. The data clearly shows that for multiple-interval scale-in approaches the arithmetic strategy is the best bet.

THE 10 PERCENT SOLUTION

An interesting trade management compromise between the low-probability, (potential) high-reward method of scaling up into a position and the high-probability, low-reward technique of scaling down into a trade is something that I call the 10 percent solution, which I picked up from a trader on one of the FX trading bulletin boards. Here is the basic strategy for this method.

Let's suppose once again that we would like to short the EUR/USD pair at 1.2500. For simplicity's sake we are willing to risk 100 points and seek a 100-point target on the trade. In other words, our stop is at 1.2600 and our target is at 1.2400. Let's further imagine that we will trade 10 mini lot contracts with total notional value of 100,000 units. We place our short at 1.2500. However, here is the rub. Instead of stopping out at 1.2600 with the whole position, we place stops at 10-point intervals for 10 percent of the position. So, if the trade moves against us by 10 points we would sell one mini lot, leaving us with nine mini lots (90,000 units) in the trade. If the trade moves 20 points counter to our entry we would sell one more mini lot, leaving us with 80,000 units—and so on until the price reached our ultimate stop-out value of 1.2600, at which point we would only have to liquidate one mini lot left in our inventory. On the opposite side we would maintain our target of 100-point profit regardless of how many lots we had left, so if we got stopped out on three mini lots but prices then turned in our favor we would harvest a 100-point profit on the remaining seven lots

Think about the implications of this strategy for a moment. In the original trade we risked 100 points on 10 mini lots or a total of 1,000 points $(100 \times 10 = 1,000)$. Using this compromise stop-out approach we were able to winnow down the total loss from 1,000 points to only 550 points if the trade became a complete bust. However, if the trade turned in our favor at any time before reaching the eighth stop-out, we would still have been able to bank a gain. The attractiveness of this approach is twofold. It automatically reduces risk if the trade moves against you, but it allows the trader to partially remain in the trade up to the very last moment. Not only is this a good practice of risk management but it is also a very clever way to get the trader to actually accept his stops. Just like a mother who feeds her baby medicine in tiny little portions in order to make it more palatable, this technique forces the trader to do what is best for his account with minimal psychological damage. Steve Cohen, probably the greatest trader in the world today—so good that he is able to charge 50 percent of gross profits in his multibillion-dollar hedge fund STC Capital—once said in an interview with Jack Schwager in *Stock Market Wizards* (Harper-Collins, 2001), "What happens when you are short a stock that is moving against you, and there is no imminent catalyst? I always tell my traders, 'If you think you're wrong, or if the market is moving against you and you don't know why, take in half. You can always put it on again.'"

When I first read that comment it went "in one ear and out the other." But upon further reflection I realized that Steve Cohen was practicing just this type of risk control methodology for all of his trading.

The 10 percent solution strategy is only a template. We need not scale out at every 10 percent of the distance to the ultimate stop. We could use

TABLE 9.2 Ten Percent Solution Strategy

Number of Profitable Lots (out of 10 Total)	Total Points at 10 Percent	Total Points at 10 Percent with Adjustable Targets
10	1,000	1,000
9	890	810
8	770	610
7	640	430
6	500	260
5	350	100
4	190	−50
3	20	−170
2	−160	−300
1	−350	−420
0	−550	−550

20 percent, 25 percent, 33 percent, or any other type of ratio that makes sense. The strategy can also be refined further to enhance the probability of success, though at a cost to profitability. For example, instead of keeping the profit target at a static 100 points from original entry, we could adjust the target in response to price action. If the price moved 10 points against our position we could reduce the profit target by 10 points, so that instead of 1.2400, we would decrease the profit target for our short to 1.2410; if the price moved 20 points we would decrease the profit target to 1.2420. Table 9.2 shows what happens when the system is adjusted in such manner.

Note that while the profitability of each trade is somewhat reduced, the probability of the success for each trade is likely to be better as it needs to travel less and less distance in order to reach the profit target.

CONCLUSION

Whenever I teach new sales traders at my firm about proper trade management in the currency market, I often start out with the example of Richard Dennis and the method of pressing the trade. Before I even have a chance to finish, some overeager rookie will inevitably jump up and confidently proclaim, "Yes! That's the *only* way to trade!" I hope this chapter has convinced you of the fallacy of such thinking. In trading there is no "only" way of doing anything, especially money management. One of the great strengths of trading is that it is an art, not a science—and there is a highly flexible discipline that allows for numerous individual modifications.

Are you comfortable with the classic 1:2 risk/reward approach? If so, it can be quite profitable, especially if you modify it as most traders do by scaling out of half of the position at profit distance equal to risk and trail the rest with a break-even stop. Do you have a killer instinct? Can you easily give up small to medium-sized gains in quest of one huge win? Then pressing the trade by constantly adding to a winning position may be the best strategy for you. What if you like taking small, frequent gains and can accept an occasional large loss? Then arithmetic scaling may be just the right approach for you to succeed. Finally, what if you are a true moderate, neither seeking remarkable gains nor afraid to absorb a series of small losses? Then the 10 percent solution may be just the "solution" for you.

As you can see, risk management trading is truly contingent on the trader's personal preferences. The currency market makes the task immeasurably easier by allowing retail traders to customize the size of their positions without incurring any marginal costs. Whether the trader wants to deal 1 million units of EUR/USD contract or only 100 units, the transaction cost among most of the reputable dealers will almost never exceed 0.03 percent. This fact allows even the smallest traders to implement any of these sophisticated risk management techniques on the exact same terms as the biggest interbank FX traders. However, the one inviolable truth that no trader, big or small, should ever forget is this: Everybody loses in trading at some time in their career. The difference between those who survive and those who do not is that winners honor their stops while losers make excuses.

CHAPTER 10

Setups!
Setups! Setups!

Technical analysis tools in and of themselves are useless. Only when we apply them to intelligent, logical trading strategies do they prove their worth and help us make money in the currency market. What follows are several trading setups designed to exploit the value of technical indicators in currency trading. These are generalized setups and by no means are a holy grail to untold riches. In fact, I can assure you that all of these setups will fail at one time or another. Hopefully, however, these trading ideas will fail intelligently; that is, either they will fail frequently but with small losses or they will fail with much larger (though not debilitating) losses but only occasionally. Regardless of the outcome, the purpose of this chapter is to show you how to use technical analysis to develop a methodical approach to trading the currency market. Why is method so important? Because it is the only way we can study, analyze, and improve our techniques. Seat-of-the-pants, instinctive trading may work well for some traders, but ultimately it is extremely limiting. In fact, this is the critical value of technical analysis—for it allows the trader to systematically apply his ideas to the market and objectively measure their success.

Some of these ideas I trade myself, while others have come from the fertile minds of friends and colleagues. However, as always, I note that no two traders are alike nor will they trade alike. Therefore I present these setups simply in the spirit of sharing. Feel free to experiment and modify any of these strategies to accommodate your tastes or preferences. Just remember to stay true to the logic of whatever strategy you devise. In trading currencies, everybody is wrong sometimes. The difference between professionals and amateurs is that professionals accept this reality while amateurs do not and are therefore doomed to be destroyed by it.

TREND DETECTION/TREND EXHAUSTION WITH BOLLINGER BANDS

When does a trend start? For some traders a new trend begins when the old trend ends. The swing high or low of the prior trend is the commencement of a move the other way and thus the birth of a new trend. For other traders, true trend must display a concerted evidence of directionality—that is, prices must make consecutive new highs or new lows for trend to be truly in place. Regardless of how one defines trend, the Bollinger band "bands" setup is one of the most flexible tools to implement either strategy.

Let's quickly review the premise behind this trade idea. The classic Bollinger bands, invented by John Bollinger, plot the standard deviation of price around the 20-period simple moving average.

The Bollinger band formula consists of the following:

BOLU = Upper Bollinger band

BOLD = Lower Bollinger band

n = Smoothing period

m = Number of standard deviations (SD)

SD = Standard deviation over last n periods

Typical price (TP) = (HI + LO + CL)/3

BOLU = MA(TP, n) + $m \times$ SD(TP, n)

BOLD = MA(TP, n) – $m \times$ SD(TP, n)

Generally we know that price tends to be range-bound 70 to 80 percent of the time. During these periods Bollinger bands serve as very accurate points of oversold or overbought value. Traders can effectively sell when prices hit the upper Bollinger band and buy when prices tag the lower Bollinger band. Note how a range-bound consolidation zone in EUR/USD provides several opportunities to sell tops and buy bottoms, harvesting nice profits for the trader. Typically the best time to trade seesaw setups is right after the price has made a major move in one direction, for as surely as day follows night, consolidation follows trend.

The basic rules to trade range are:

1. Establish at least one swing high and one swing low for the range.

2. Measure the amplitude of the range.

3. Go long the next time the price hits the lower Bollinger band.

4. Set a stop at the low of the entry bar plus half the value of the amplitude of the range.

5. Exit the long when the price hits the upper Bollinger band and immediately establish a short, placing a stop at the high of the entry bar plus one-half the value of the amplitude of the range (see Figure 10.1).

6. Make minor adjustments by recalculating the range value as it expands.

7. Repeat the process until you are stopped out.

Between April and October of 2004 this strategy worked exceedingly well in the EUR/USD pair, registering five consecutive profitable trades. To fully appreciate just how profitable this kind of trading can be, note that this method was able to bank cumulative gains of 1,000 points in an environment in which the currency pair never moved more than 300 points either way.

Why was this strategy so successful? First, it was implemented after a strong trend move as EUR/USD gained nearly 1,000 points from 2003 to

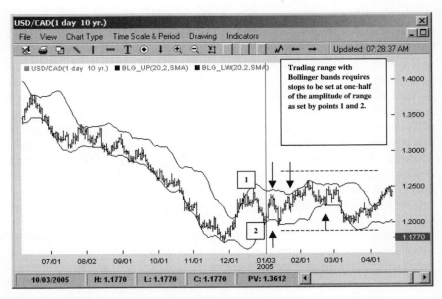

FIGURE 10.1 Trading Range with Bollinger Bands
Source: FXtrek IntelliChart™. Copyright 2001–2005 FXtrek.com, Inc.

2004. After trends prices will very often experience a long period of consolidation as the market digests and adjusts to new values. Second, the strategy used the classic money management technique to control risk. By using one-half the amplitude of the range, this trading technique provided enough room to avoid market noise while keeping the reward-to-risk ratio at 2:1. In highly range-bound markets such as that of April to October of 2004 this method was extremely profitable, but even in markets where it generated only one profitable trade before stopping the trader out, the method was a net winner because of its 2:1 reward-to-risk money management rules.

Going back to Figure 10.1, if we connect every point of entry and exit we realize that the pattern forms a Z-shaped line. Looking at this line we can see that this in fact is a horizontal trend. Although this concept may seem like an oxymoron, if we were to stretch out the Z-shaped line it would be as long and as impressive as any vertical trend. Thus we can see that trends need not be vertical to be profitable. Horizontal price action, boring as it may seem to an untrained eye, can be a gold mine to an astute trader using Bollinger bands and proper money management to trade them.

TREND TRADING WITH BB BANDS

Although the classic use of Bollinger bands is to trade range, Bollinger bands can be extremely effective in trading trend as well. I already introduced you to the concept of Bollinger band "bands" in Chapter 5, but let's review the idea once more. In the Bollinger band "bands" setup the trader superimposes two sets of Bollinger bands. First he lays down the standard Bollinger bands set to 2 standard deviations and then he applies another set of BB's set to only 1 standard deviation. The result of this exercise is that the trader now has access to a set of very accurate dynamic trend channels. If the price trades in between the two upper Bollinger bands it's in an uptrend; if the price trades in between the two lower Bollinger bands it's in a downtrend. If it trades somewhere in between the two channels it's considered to be in no-man's-land and trendless (see Figure 10.2).

Bollinger band "bands" can be used both as a trend detection tool and as a trend exhaustion tool. Let's first take a look at how we can use the Bollinger band "bands" to spot trend exhaustion and consider several trading tactics to take advantage of such a setup. If trend is defined as price trading between the two Bollinger bands, then price leaving the BB

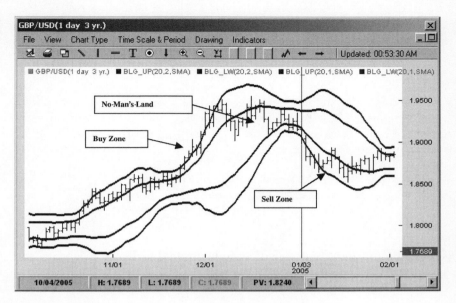

FIGURE 10.2 Trend Exhaustion with Bollinger Band "Bands"
Source: FXtrek IntelliChart™. Copyright 2001–2005 FXtrek.com, Inc.

channel connotes trend exhaustion. The Bollinger band "bands" trend exhaustion setup is fairy straightforward.

1. The price must trade within either upper or lower Bollinger band "band."
2. If the closing price of the period is either above the preceding Bollinger band sell channel or below the preceding Bollinger band buy channel, a trend exhaustion signal is generated.
3. In the case of a sell channel break, the trader would buy at market at the start of the next bar, and in the case of a break of a buy channel the trader would sell at market at the start of the next bar.

Here is where the trade becomes very interesting, depending on the tactics the trader employs. The simplest approach is to put on the trade and place a stop in the case of long at the swing low minus 1 point and minus the spread, which would exit the trade if the swing low was broken. The target on the trade would be the opposite Bollinger band (see Figure 10.3).

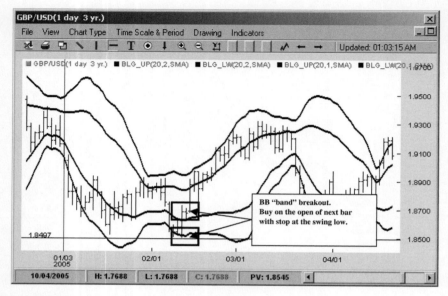

FIGURE 10.3 Bollinger Band "Band" Trade with Price Stop
Source: FXtrek IntelliChart™. Copyright 2001–2005 FXtrek.com, Inc.

Although this type of trade will generate many stop-outs as prices rarely make V-shaped bottoms, it carries a very favorable reward-to-risk structure. Note that in Figure 10.3 the risk is only 50 points but the reward is 200 points. The trader can be wrong three out of four trades and still be profitable under such circumstances.

Another technique to this setup would call for the following game plan:

1. Enter the setup at market when the trend exhaustion signal is given.
2. Place a stop below the swing low.
3. Liquidate one-third of the position when the price reaches the 20-period simple moving average (20 SMA).
4. Place stop at break-even point.
5. Liquidate one-third of the position at the tag of the opposing 2 standard deviation bollinger band.
6. If the price decides to climb the Bollinger band channel, liquidate the final one-third of the position if the price bar closes outside of the Bollinger band channel zone.

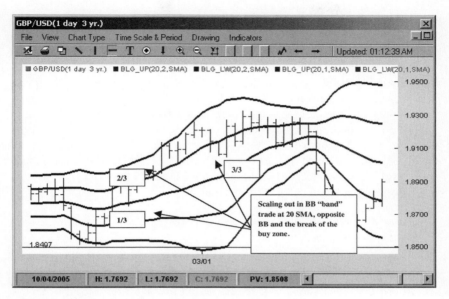

FIGURE 10.4   Scaling Out of Bollinger Band "Band" Trade
Source: FXtrek IntelliChart™. Copyright 2001–2005 FXtrek.com, Inc.

This technique is designed to dynamically adapt to various market conditions (see Figure 10.4). Under this strategy a trader will get stopped out for a relatively small loss if the price fails to make a turn or he will harvest a modest profit if the price makes a reflex retracement to the 20-period simple moving average. On occasion when prices make a strong move to the opposite Bollinger band, the trader will bank meaningful profits on two-thirds of his position. Finally, in those very rare instances when the price makes a V-shaped bottom and generates a very strong countertrend, the trader has the opportunity to collect massive profits on part of his position. Essentially by gradually scaling out of the position a trader can take advantage of every possible scenario that the market may present. The malleability of this approach is its most attractive feature.

VOLATILITY STOP

One of the problems with the prior techniques is the large number of stop-outs they tend to generate. Prices will very frequently exceed their swing highs or swing lows if for no other reason than the fact that dealers are well aware of those price points and will make stop-hunting forays to collect easy profits. What happens next can be very disheartening as the price makes a turn in the original direction but the trader is taken out of what ultimately becomes a winning position. For traders who are psychologically comfortable with multiple small stops, the approaches listed earlier present little problem. But for traders like myself, who absolutely cannot stand a constant series of small losses but are more than willing to accept an occasional large loss, the following strategy to trade trend exhaustion with Bollinger band "bands" may be a much better approach. Instead of using a hard price stop, this method uses a volatility stop generated off the Bollinger bands themselves (see Figure 10.5).

Here are the basic rules for this setup.

1. Enter the setup with one-half position size at market when the trend exhaustion signal is given.

2. At the point of entry measure the distance between the Bollinger band +1 standard deviation and –1 standard deviation.

3. Add the value from step 2 to the swing low if trading long or to the swing high if trading short.

4. Place stop at that point.

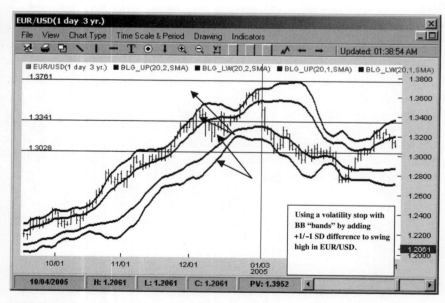

FIGURE 10.5 Bollinger Band "Band" Trade with Volatility Stop
Source: FXtrek IntelliChart™. Copyright 2001–2005 FXtrek.com, Inc.

5. If trade moves to profit, exit at the opposite Bollinger band.
6. If trade moves against you, add the second half of the position on the next tag of the 2 standard deviation Bollinger band.
7. Exit the full trade on the tag of the opposite Bollinger band.

This is a trading tactic that uses a highly probative approach to price action. It assumes that the trend channel break signal provided by the Bollinger bands is simply a clue rather than an exact sign of trend exhaustion. As such, it uses a wide stop and a scale-in approach that materially improves the reward-to-risk odds and increases the probabilities of success as well.

Why use the bandwidth of +1 SD to –1 SD of Bollinger bands as a stop-out value? Because Bollinger bands by their essence measure volatility. Therefore, in highly volatile markets Bollinger bands will be naturally wide while in low-volatility markets they will be quite compressed. In other words, by using this type of dynamic volatility stop the trader will be able to respond to the present market conditions rather than impose uniform risk-control measures over highly diverse market environments. Note, for example, how in Figure 10.6 this method generates a tight stop causing minimal damage when the setup fails, but in Figure 10.7 this setup

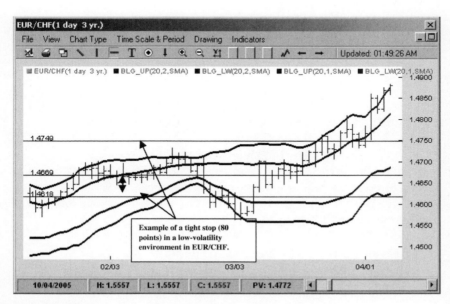

FIGURE 10.6 Low-Volatility Stop with Bollinger Band "Bands"
Source: FXtrek IntelliChart™. Copyright 2001–2005 FXtrek.com, Inc.

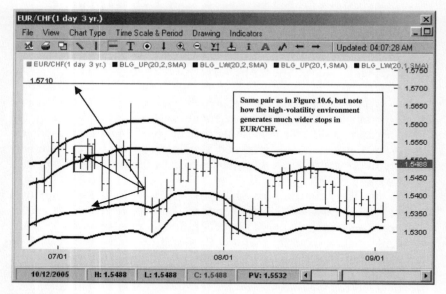

FIGURE 10.7 High-Volatility Stop with Bollinger Band "Bands"
Source: FXtrek IntelliChart™. Copyright 2001–2005 FXtrek.com, Inc.

uses a wide stop that keeps the trader in the trade until it eventually turns around and becomes profitable.

TRADING PURE TREND WITH BOLLINGER BANDS

As we have already seen, Bollinger band "bands" present a trend trader with an elegant natural way to draft trend channels and therefore present several interesting trend trading setups. The simplest and purest setup follows these rules (see Figure 10.8). (Note that these describe a long setup, but the rules for shorts are simply reversed.)

1. Price must enter the Bollinger band buy zone.
2. Price should close within the buy zone to trigger a buy signal.
3. Place stop at the bottom of the entry bar.
4. If the trade moves in the right direction, exit only when price closes below the buy channel.

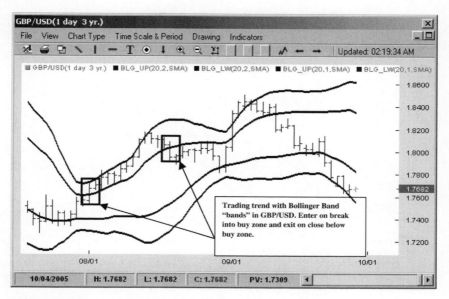

FIGURE 10.8 Trading Trend with Bollinger Band "Bands"
Source: FXtrek IntelliChart™. Copyright 2001–2005 FXtrek.com, Inc.

This is a pure trend setup that strictly follows the trend trader's most important dictum: "Either I am right or I am out." Trend trading is a clear-cut methodology. Prices must continue to trend or there is no logical reason to remain in the trade. This is why this setup has a very tight stop. Once trend is established, though, a trend trader wants to give it plenty of leeway to fully bloom. As long as prices remain within the uptrend channel the trend trader maintains his position. Note that the stop-out rules of the setup call for prices to close below the uptrend channel rather than merely pierce it. This condition prevents too many early stop-outs, as price will often test the lower bounds of the channel. However if bulls are able to close the bar within the channel that type of price action would suggest that directional power is still tilted to the upside. Note also that just like busy office workers hopping on and off an elevator, trend traders can reenter the trend many times during a significant move as conditions turn favorable. Figure 10.9 shows a good example of just such a setup. Between October and December of 2004 the EUR/USD climbed 1,300 points. Several times during this move prices fell out of the uptrend channel, but persistent trend traders could have rejoined the bulls once price resumed the uptrend and would have captured large pieces of the move.

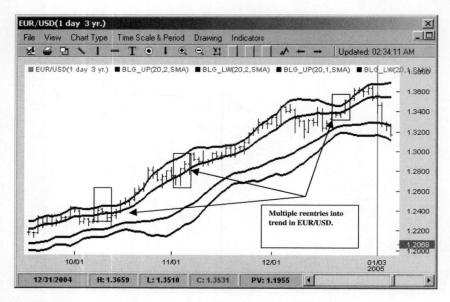

FIGURE 10.9 Multiple Trend Entries with Bollinger Band "Bands"
Source: FXtrek IntelliChart™. Copyright 2001–2005 FXtrek.com, Inc.

SCALPING TO TREND

Another interesting setup for more short-oriented traders also involves Bollinger band "bands" and allows traders to exploit the interplay between the 1 and 2 standard deviation bands. Here is how this trade sets up, and again I will use a long example with rules simply reversed for the short side.

1. Price enters the buy channel and tags the upper 2 standard deviation Bollinger band.
2. If price retraces down to 1 standard deviation Bollinger band, buy at market.
3. Place stop at 20-period SMA.
4. Exit trade on next tag of 2 standard deviation Bollinger band.
5. Repeat process.

This is a very interesting setup because it utilizes both fading and trending techniques to make several quick high-probability trades. The

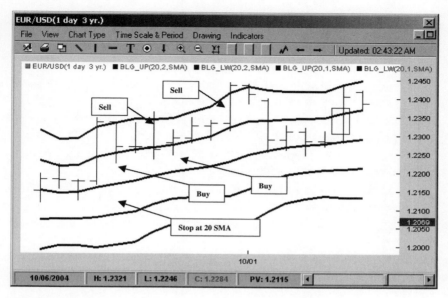

FIGURE 10.10 Scalping to Trend with Bollinger Band "Bands"
Source: FXtrek IntelliChart™. Copyright 2001–2005 FXtrek.com, Inc.

idea behind this setup is that the underlying power of the move lies with the direction of the trend. Therefore, by absorbing the opposite side of any profit-taking move, the trader enters the trend at a favorable price and has a quick opportunity to bank profit on the next wave up. Note in Figure 10.10 how a nimble scalper is able to generate 300 points of gains before finally getting stopped out, while a more long-term trader is able to harvest only 100 points of profit.

THE MACD TURN

Oscillators come in all shapes and sizes, but for my money nothing beats the MACD histogram for sheer simplicity or accuracy. The MACD turn, which is a setup I like to trade on anything from as small as 15-minute bar charts to as large as weekly candlesticks graphs, operates on a deceptively simple premise but actually uses rather fancy money management to turn it into success. The basic premise of the MACD turn is this: Momentum precedes price. That means in a battle between price and momentum always trust momentum.

Here is the setup in a nutshell (see Figure 10.11).

1. Overlay Bollinger band "bands" on a chart using 20 SMA, 2 standard deviation, and 1 standard deviation settings.
2. Overlay the MACD histogram using standard MACD settings of 9-period exponential moving average (EMA) and 12-period EMA.
3. For short setups, price must be in the upper Bollinger band channel; for long setups, price must be in the lower Bollinger band channel.
4. For a short setup look for the MACD histogram to print a lower high bar indicating that momentum is waning.
5. Measure the distance between the low of the most recent bar and the most recent swing high.
6. Place a sell stop at halfway between the two points for one-third of total position.
7. If the trade is triggered, set a take-profit target at 20-period SMA.
8. If price moves in the opposite direction of the trade and makes new swing highs but MACD histogram does not, sell another one-third of the position at market.

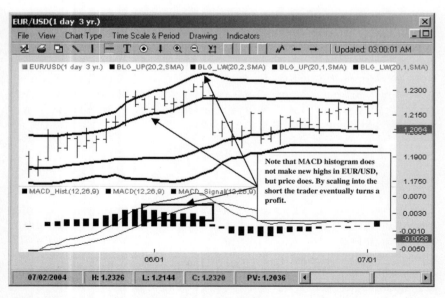

FIGURE 10.11 Trading MACD Histogram Rather Than Price
Source: FXtrek IntelliChart™. Copyright 2001–2005 FXtrek.com, Inc.

9. If price continues to move higher but MACD histogram has not exceeded new highs, sell final one-third of the position on next tag of upper Bollinger band.

10. Stop out only if MACD histogram makes a new high.

11. Reverse all steps for long setup.

As you can see, the MACD turn setup requires a lot of fancy money management but it does adhere to one simple trading rule—the trader enters the trade off an indicator trigger and exits the trade off an indicator trigger. One of the critical mistakes that many technically oriented traders make is to use an indicator-based entry but a price-based stop. This is the trading equivalent of comparing apples to oranges. The MACD turn was designed specifically to eliminate this problem.

As I've noted many times before, FX is one of the most active stop-hunting markets in the world. Dealers will always want to probe recent highs and new lows just to test out market sentiment and to pick up cheap inventory on the buy side as well as get rid of expensive product on the sell side. Therefore price in FX will often take out the swing highs or swing lows, sometimes by only a few points but sometimes by several hundred. The great value of the MACD turn is that it does not allow the trader to fall for this common bluff. As long as momentum does not reach new highs, the trader continues to scale into the trade and thereby achieves a better blended price.

The MACD turn, the way I trade it, is a very labor-intensive setup. It requires a lot of trade management to actively scale against the position and then quickly take off trades at the first sign of profit. Often I will even cover the most recent trade with the position and will go short or long once again if an opportunity presents itself. This setup the way I trade it can also suffer hideous losses. Basically the MACD turn with the scale-in approach manufactures many small profits but occasionally produces very large losses if prices never turn. Just like an insurance company that hopes to offset its few large losses by collecting many premiums (for all those in the insurance business—yes, I know it's not a perfect analogy, but please indulge me), the MACD turn follows the same business plan.

There are different ways to trade the same idea that may be more suitable for your style and risk profile. One interesting way to trade the MACD turn is to use a money management approach that is antithetical to the one I use. Instead of using a partial scale-in strategy, a trader can enter the position all at once, but in the case of a short trade, if the price made a new swing high on the next bar the trader would scale out of the position one-third of the total value at a time. This strategy may be very useful to traders uncomfortable with the idea of increasing risk as prices move against their positions. Instead of suffering ever-larger floating losses from adverse price movement, this method deleverages the trading account while at the same time allowing part of the trade to remain on the books in case of eventual turnaround to profit.

THE TAO OF RSI

The Relative Strength Index (RSI) is another indicator that works exceedingly well in the FX market, and it does so on all time levels from 15-minute charts to daily or even weekly graphs. As I've noted earlier in the book, there are myriad ways to trade RSI. Some traders even use it as a proxy for volume since volume is not reported in spot FX. They view a rapid increase in RSI much like they would a rapid increase in volume as a precursor to further price movement. Other traders will prefer to trade the RSI graph rather than the price graph because they believe that the normalization process of RSI provides a truer, more accurate picture of price action.

This setup is more straightforward than some of these methods. The Tao of RSI simply uses the original purpose of the indicator to find overbought and oversold areas and pick short-term tops and bottoms (see Figure 10.12).

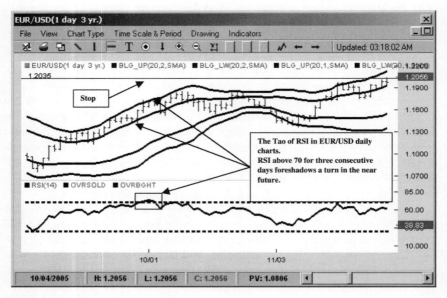

FIGURE 10.12 The Tao of RSI
Source: FXtrek IntelliChart™. Copyright 2001–2005 FXtrek.com, Inc.

Here are the rules:

1. Lay out Bollinger band "bands" on a price graph (Bollingers with 20 SMA 2 SD and Bollingers with 20 SMA 1 SD).
2. Plot RSI with standard setting of (14,1).
3. If the price chart prints three consecutive bars with RSI readings of 70 or greater, short on the close of the third bar.
4. Measure from the bottom of the first bar to the top of the third bar.
5. Add that distance to the top of the third bar and place a stop there.

For a long setup the rules are:

1. Lay out Bollinger band "bands" on a price graph (Bollingers with 20 SMA 2 SD and Bollingers with 20 SMA 1 SD).
2. Plot RSI with standard setting of (14,1).
3. If the price chart prints three consecutive bars with RSI readings of 30 or less, go long on the close of the third bar.
4. Measure from the bottom of the first bar to the top of the third bar.
5. Add that distance to the bottom of the third bar and place a stop there.

The exit rules for this setup can vary. Here are some possibilities:

1. If the price moves in your direction by the value of your stop (i.e., if you risked 100 points on the trade and it has moved 100 points in your favor), move your stop to the break-even point and target the opposite 2 standard deviation Bollinger band as exit.

This approach is the most aggressive and will result in many stop-outs and scratch trades, as it is very difficult to pick exact turns in the market. The risk/reward on this type of trade, however, will be superb, as the winning trades may likely generate three to four times the amount of points of losing trades, depending on the market volatility.

2. If the price moves in your direction by 70 percent the value of your stop (i.e., if you risked 100 points on the trade and it has moved 70 points in your favor), take profit on one-half of the position, move your stop to the break-even point, and target the opposite 2 standard deviation Bollinger band as exit for the rest.

This is the compromise approach that tries to harvest some profit right away, but allows the trader to benefit partially from a large turn in the market. It provides the psychological benefit of banking some profits quickly, which allows the trader to bask in the glow of a somewhat profitable trade, but at the expense of minimizing the full profit potential if the trade turns into a big winner.

3. If the price moves in your direction by 70 percent of the value of your stop (i.e., if you risked 100 points on the trade and it has moved 70 points in your favor), take full profit on the position.

This method will never produce outsized profits, but it is the highest-probability method of all three. For traders who don't mind building their fortune a nickel at a time, this may be the best approach as it tries to pinpoint the most oversold and overbought points on the price chart and then quickly skim off any retracement profits that occur. Note, however, that this strategy needs to be at least 60 percent accurate in order to make money.

Assume you make 10 trades, each with a 100-point stop. Six trades make 70 points for a total of 420 points, and four lose 100 points each for –400. The total would be a net profit of 20 points. If the trader was successful 70 percent of the time, the net profit would be 190 points [$(7 \times 70) - (3 \times 100)$]—showing the critical role of high probability in the success of this trading method.

The example also brings out a very important consideration that many novice traders overlook when testing these strategies. When measuring the efficacy of all these ideas it is very important to stay consistent in your trade time frames. For example, in the statement that the strategy requires 60 percent accuracy in order to be profitable, the implied assumption is that the trader will trade all 10 trades on the same time frame, which in the case of 100-point stops will most likely be the daily chart. Imagine, however, a trader who decides to trade this setup on a 15-minute chart risking 15 points for a 10-point target. He makes eight consecutive winning trades, harvesting 80 points of profit. Then emboldened by his success he moves over to a daily chart and decides to risk 100 points for a 70-point target. Unfortunately, the trade is a loser and he is stopped out. His total position after eight successful trades and one unsuccessful trade is a 20-point loss. Furious, the trader stops trading this idea, convinced that it doesn't work.

Unfortunately, this type of sloppy thinking is very prevalent among many new traders. The quest for easy money makes many novices abandon valuable technical tools before they properly learn how to use them.

Turning back to the Tao of RSI, however, we can see how effective this setup can be on any time frame.

Figure 10.13 shows the trade in AUD/USD on a 15-minute chart, while Figure 10.14 uses a daily graph. In both cases the RSI is able to accurately pinpoint the extremes and allow traders to make profitable turn trades.

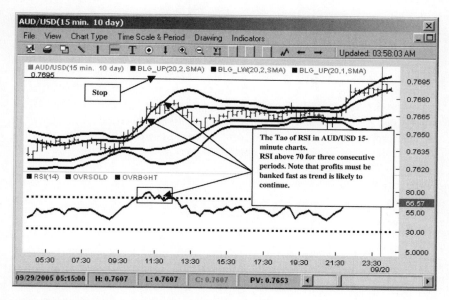

FIGURE 10.13 The Tao of RSI 15-Minute Chart
Source: FXtrek IntelliChart™. Copyright 2001–2005 FXtrek.com, Inc.

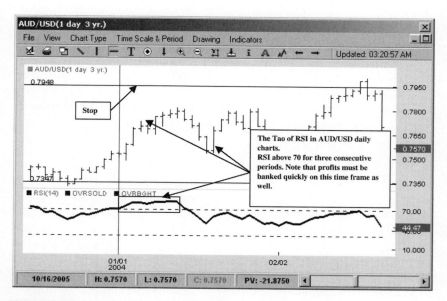

FIGURE 10.14 The Tao of RSI Daily Chart
Source: FXtrek IntelliChart™. Copyright 2001–2005 FXtrek.com, Inc.

TREND DETECTION WITH THREE SIMPLE MOVING AVERAGES

Up to now, I have shown you mainly trend exhaustion or turn setups. Part of the reason lies in my own contrarian nature, as I simply find it difficult to trade with the crowd. The other part is simply due to the fact that I genuinely find trend exhaustion easier to spot and trade. After all, it is easy to see a trend on a chart. However, once a trend is identified there are only three possibilities for where the price may go:

1. Continuation
2. Consolidation
3. Reversal

Of the three choices, two can be successfully traded with trend exhaustion methods, providing a nice probability edge, which is why I am much more comfortable trading those strategies. There is, however, one low-risk trend method that I like very much, and it comprises my final setup.

Here are the rules for the three simple moving average (3 SMA) setup (see Figure 10.15):

1. Place 7-period, 20-period, and 65-period simple moving averages on the chart.
2. Wait until volatility declines and 7, 20, and 65 SMAs all compress together.
3. As price breaks out in either direction watch for the 3 SMAs to fan out with the 7 above the 20 and the 20 above the 65 in the case of a long, and the 7 below the 20 and the 20 below the 65 in the case of a short.
4. In the case of a long buy, as price retraces to the 7 SMA, place a stop a few points below the 65 SMA.
5. Exit the trade when the 7 SMA crosses the 20 SMA.

In and of themselves moving averages are notoriously poor indicators because by definition they lag price action and send late signals that are vulnerable to whipsaws. However, the three simple moving average filter is designed to place the trader on the right side of the trend by making sure that short-term, intermediate-term, and long-term price forces are all aligned in the same direction. Furthermore, because this setup waits for low volatility environments it assumes very little risk for a potentially large reward. Price action itself can be very noisy. By showing the average price movement on the short-term, intermediate-term, and longer-term time frames, the 3 SMA

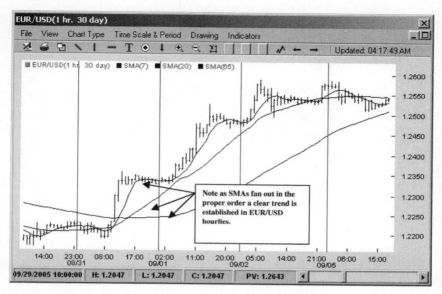

FIGURE 10.15 Three Simple Moving Average "Fan Out"
Source: FXtrek IntelliChart™. Copyright 2001–2005 FXtrek.com, Inc.

setup can reveal the underlying direction that may not be visible through pure price action alone. The setup is still prone to stop-outs, but as Figures 10.16 and 10.17 show, when it catches the move the profits are large.

CONCLUSION

Technical analysis is a wonderful tool. Academics scoff at the value of indicators and chart patterns, blithely dismissing all price movement as random; but most real-life traders find technical analysis critical to their success. It is very difficult to mount an effective intellectual argument against the academics. To buttress their argument, researchers like to use fancy words such as stationarity (meaning that every time element in a series is independent of those preceding it) along with reams of statistical data to prove their points. On a practical level, however, the performance of thousands of technically oriented traders contradicts their thesis.

One simple example of how academic exercise is so far removed from the real world is the common assumption among academicians that any given trade has a 50 percent chance of success. I'll never forget a

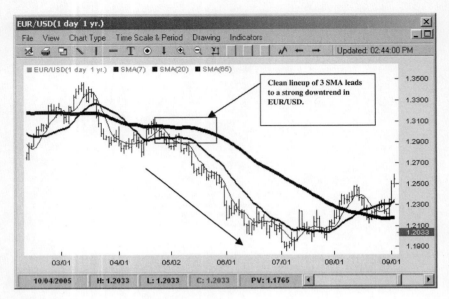

FIGURE 10.16   3 SMA Short in EUR/USD
Source: FXtrek IntelliChart™. Copyright 2001–2005 FXtrek.com, Inc.

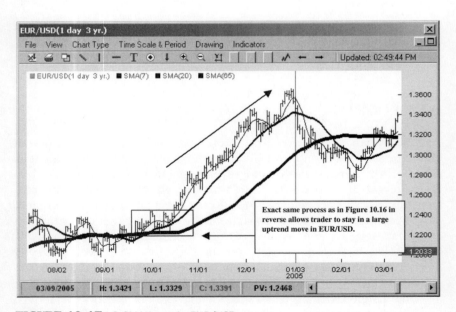

FIGURE 10.17   3 SMA Long in EUR/USD
Source: FXtrek IntelliChart™. Copyright 2001–2005 FXtrek.com, Inc.

conversation I once had with Tom Sarnoff, who runs an options broker-age boutique called thinkorswin.com and prior to that was one of the biggest market makers on the floor of the Chicago Board Options Exchange. Tom, a true trader, once noted that while most novices approach the market thinking that their odds of success are 50–50, the actual odds are probably more like 25–75 against them.

Why? Because markets are driven not by some random number–generating machine, but by very skilled and wily human beings who constantly try to trap, bluff, and sucker newbies into losing their capital. Tom's insight explained several things. First, it demonstrates that almost all mechanical systems are doomed to fail or at the very least to trade very poorly for extended periods of time. Why? Because all systems are optimized for either range trading or trend trading. Once the environment changes they inevitably begin to degrade. Much like a frog that gets cooked in gradually hotter water, the systems are unable to adjust to the change in market conditions until it is too late.

Tom's point also explains a lot about my own journey. When I started trading seven years ago as a clueless newbie I remember a particularly nasty string of 12 consecutive losing trades followed by a cruel reprieve of one win and then an additional 10 losses. As I started to write this book in earnest in July 2005 I decided to actively day trade both my futures account in which I trade the E-mini Dow Jones index and my spot FX account in which I trade mainly the major pairs. I did this basically to see, as the saying in the software business goes, if I would eat my own dogfood—in other words, if I could trade successfully with technical analysis while I was writing a book on the subject. In the futures account I made 91 trades with 83 winners. In FX I made 46 trades and 42 of those were winners. So in seven years I went from generating a record of 1 win and 22 losses to compiling a string of 125 wins and 12 losses.

Now, does this prove anything? No, of course not. Any moderately knowledgeable analyst could make mincemeat of my data. For one, my few losses were much larger than my many wins. For another, my maximum adverse excursion (the amount I allowed positions to move against me) almost always exceeded my maximum gains. In the end I ended net positive in both accounts, making approximately 3 percent in futures and 16 percent in my currency account over that time frame. Still, any skilled statistician could easily argue that I was just lucky and the statistician may well be correct. But let's look at what I did differently this time versus my early years.

- I used technical analysis to pinpoint overbought and oversold areas and traded only when a specific setup appeared on the chart.
- I utilized risk management tactics that were in sync with my personality, which in my case called for taking profits very quickly. This type of

trading generated many small wins and a few large losses that I was psychologically willing to accept.

- Once I developed my setups I was highly methodical in my approach—having thought through every possible scenario to the end. I knew exactly where I would get out on my winners and also what market conditions would force me to fold and accept my losers. I even had a plan for what I would do when my Internet connection would inevitably crash.

That's it. It's as simple as that. Comparing the results of my early years to my trading now, the single biggest difference can be summarized in one word: organization. The most random aspect of my early trading wasn't price action, but my own behavior. My responses to the market, like those of most novice traders, were wildly illogical and highly inconsistent. "The fault, dear Brutus, is not in our stars, but in ourselves," as Shakespeare once wrote in *Julius Caesar.*

This is the primary reason why technical analysis is so valuable to trading. It systematizes and categorizes price data, allowing the trader to recognize discernible repetitive patterns. Technical analysis cannot guarantee success. It cannot accurately predict the next move. At best it can foreshadow and offer clues to future direction, most notably when momentum diverges from price action. This is the crux of its value. Yet for many skilled traders that is enough to provide a meaningful and profitable edge.

Success in trading can be summarized with three C's—confidence, consistency, and compounding. Confidence comes only from failure. That may sound convoluted, but allow me to explain. Confidence in trading is a direct result of experience. A trader needs to put on many trades—perhaps thousands of trades—before he will be comfortable and confident in his approach. He needs to see repetitive price patterns through a variety of market environments before he can develop the courage to consistently enter trades with strong expectation of profit. The sheer nature of this process implies that traders need to make many mistakes in order to acclimate themselves to the vagaries of the market. Thus confidence breeds consistency, and consistency leads to compounding of returns, which is the only path to wealth.

Trading with technical analysis, like any great vocation in life, is a never-ending study of self and the world around you. The currency market, with its massive liquidity, complete customization of size, and round-the-clock markets, makes this enterprise only that much more attractive. I truly enjoy the journey every day. I hope you will, as well.

Glossary

account A record of transactions of goods and services owed to one person by another.

ADX. *See* **Average Directional Index**.

agent An intermediary or person hired to carry out transactions on behalf of another person.

aggregate demand Total demand in an economy, consisting of government spending, private/consumer purchasing, and business investment.

all or none Refers to requests for a broker to fill an order completely at a predetermined price or not at all. Refers to both buy and sell orders.

anonymous trading Visible bids and offers on the market without the identity of the bidder and seller being revealed. Anonymous trades allow the high-profile investors to execute transactions without the scrutiny of the whole market.

appreciation An increase in the value of a currency in response to market demand.

arbitrage A riskless opportunity to profit, with no uncertainty involved. In the foreign exchange market, arbitrage arises when a profit can be made by locking in differentials in exchange rates of identical currency pairs. For example, a trader who is able to execute equal-amount purchases of GBP/USD and USD/JPY against a sale of GBP/JPY for a profit would be engaging in arbitrage. Arbitrage opportunities in the foreign exchange market are rare.

ascending triangle A bullish continuation pattern that is shaped like a right triangle consisting of two or more equal highs forming a horizontal line at the top.

ask rate   The lowest price at which a financial instrument will be offered for sale, such as the bid/ask spread in the foreign exchange market.

ask size   The number of units a seller is willing to sell at his/her ask rate.

asset allocation   The diversification of one's assets into different sectors, such as real estate, stocks, bonds, and forex, to optimize growth potential and minimize risk.

asset swap   An interest-rate swap used to alter the cash flow characteristics of an institution's assets in order to provide a better match with its liabilities.

attorney in fact   A person given the right or authority to act on behalf of another to carry out business transactions and implement documents.

authorized forex dealer   A financial institution or bank authorized to deal in foreign exchange.

Aussie   Term for Australian dollar.

Average Directional Index (ADX)   Unlike most oscillators, ADX does not attempt to gauge the direction of the trend; instead, it works to gauge the strength of the trend. ADX operates on a scale of 0 to 100; the higher the oscillator, the stronger the trend. Typically readings of 20 or higher indicate presence of trend.

away from the market   When the bid on an order is lower (or the ask price is higher) than the current market price for the security traded.

back office   Refers to the administrative departments of financial service companies, which carry out and confirm financial transactions. Duties include accounting, settlements, clearances, regulatory compliance, and record maintenance.

back-testing   The process of designing a trading strategy to be tested on historical data of the financial instrument. Most technical analysis strategies are tested via this approach.

balance/account balance   The net value of an account.

balance of payments   A record of all transactions made by one particular country with the rest of the world. It compares the amount of economic activity between a specific country and all other countries within a certain period. This number includes trade balance, foreign investments, and investments by foreigners.

balance of trade   Net flow of goods (exports minus imports) between two countries.

Bank for International Settlements (BIS)   An international organization fostering the cooperation of central banks and international financial institutions. BIS, located in Basel, Switzerland, is essentially a central bank for central banks. It monitors and collects data on international banking activity and promulgates rules concerning international bank regulation.

bar chart   On a daily bar chart each bar represents one day's activity. The vertical bar is drawn from the day's highest price to the day's lowest price. Opening price and closing price are represented by marks on the bar to the left and right, respectively.

base currency   In general terms, currency in which an investor or issuer maintains its book of accounts. In the FX markets, the base currency is the first currency of the currency pair, meaning that quotes are usually expressed as one U.S. dollar per the other currency. USD/JPY = 120 would mean that one dollar would purchase 120 yen. The primary exceptions to this rule are the British pound, the euro, and the Australian dollar, which are quoted as EUR/USD, GBP/USD, and AUD/USD.

basis   The difference between the cash price and the futures price.

basis point   Measure of a bond's yield equal to 1/100th of 1 percent. A 1 percent change in yield is equal to 100 basis points, and 0.01 percent is equal to one basis point.

bear   Investor acting on the belief that prices will decline.

bear market   Any market that exhibits a declining trend. Typically bear markets are defined as declines of 20 percent or more from peak to trough.

bear trap   A bear trap occurs when prices break below a significant level and generate a sell signal, but then reverse direction and hence invalidate the sell signal. Bear traps serve as opportunities for reversal traders, whereas trend/momentum traders suffer losses due to the whipsaw change in direction.

bid   The price an investor is willing to pay for an asset.

bid/ask spread   The difference between the bid price and the ask price.

big figure   Refers to the first number to the left of the decimal point in an exchange rate quote, which changes so infrequently that dealers often omit them in quotes. For example, EUR/USD may be trading 1.2000 by 1.2003 with 1 considered to be the big figure.

Bollinger bands   An indicator that allows users to compare volatility and relative price levels over a period of time. This indicator consists of three bands designed to encompass the majority of a security's price action: a simple moving average in the middle; an upper band 2 standard deviations away from the simple moving average (usually set to a time frame of 20); and a corresponding lower band that is also 2 standard deviations away from the moving average. Since the band width is a function of standard deviation, assets with greater volatility will have wider bands.

bonds   Debt instrument used to raise capital, issued for a period greater than one year. Bondholders are loaning money (investing in debt) to companies and governments for a defined period of time, at the end of which they will be repaid the principal and paid a specified interest rate. Bond prices are inversely related to interest rates; as interest rates rise, bond prices fall. There are numerous types of bonds, including Treasury bonds and notes, municipal bonds, and corporate bonds.

book   Recording of the total positions held by a trader or desk.

Bretton Woods Accord   This 1944 accord established a fixed exchange rate regime, whose aim was to provide stability in the world economy after the Great Depression and World War II. The agreement fixed the exchange rates of major currencies to the U.S. dollar and set the price of gold to $35. It required central bank intervention to maintain the fixed exchange rates. The U.S. central bank was required to exchange dollars for gold, which eventually led to the demise of this system when the demand for the dollar declined, forcing President Richard Nixon to stop the exchange of dollars for gold, effectively ending the system in 1971.

broker   Individual or firm acting as an intermediary to bring together buyers and sellers typically for a commission or fee.

bull   Investor who expects markets to rise.

bull market   A market where prices are rising.

bull trap   The opposite of a bear trap; occurs when indicators suggest an uptrend, but the market reverses its momentum and begins to decline once more.

Bundesbank/Buba   Central bank of Germany—the largest economy in European Union.

buy a bounce   A recommendation to initiate a long trade if the price bounces from a certain level.

buy break   A recommendation to buy the currency pair if it breaks the current level specified.

buy stops above   A recommendation to enter the market when the exchange rate breaks through a specific level. The client placing a stop entry order believes that when the market's momentum breaks through a specified level, the rate will continue to move in that direction.

cable   Term used to describe the exchange rate between the U.S. dollar and the British pound.

candlestick chart   Identical to a bar chart in the information conveyed, but presented in an entirely different visual context. The candlestick encapsulates the open, high, low, and close of the trading period in a single candle. If the close is above the open, the actual candle is either hollow or green in color. If the close is below the open, the actual candle is filled in or red in color.

capital markets   Markets in which capital (stocks, bonds, etc.) are traded.

carry trade   An investment strategy of buying a higher-yielding currency with the capital of a lower-yielding currency to gain an interest rate differential. In late 2005 the NZD/JPY pair serves as a classic example of a carry trade. With the New Zealand dollar yielding 7.25 percent and the yen yielding 0 percent, the investor would in effect be able to generate a 7.25 percent rate of return from interest rate differentials but would of course be exposed to any capital depreciation risk should the exchange rate decline.

central bank   A banking organization, usually independent of government, responsible for the control and production of the country's monetary stock and implementation of the country's monetary policy.

channel   An upward or downward trend whose boundaries are marked by two straight lines. A break above/below the channel lines signals a potential change in the trend.

chartist   Refers to a technical analyst or one who analyzes charts/graphs and data to uncover potential trends and price patterns.

clearing Refers to the confirmation and final settlement of trades.

close a position (position squaring) Refers to getting rid of a position by either buying back a short position or selling a long position.

commission A fee charged by a broker or an agent for carrying out transactions/orders.

confirmation A written document verifying the completion of a trade/transaction to include such things as date, fees or commissions, settlement terms, and price.

confirmation on a chart A subsequent indicator or chart pattern, following an initial alert for a trade opportunity, which serves to legitimize the initial alert. Confirmation of a trade is believed to reduce the risk associated with that trade by forcing the trader to comply with more rigorous conditions before putting on a position.

contagion Term used to describe the spread of economic crises from one country to another within close geographic proximity. This term was first used following the Asian financial crisis in 1997, which began in Thailand and soon spread to other East Asian economies. It subsequently has been used to refer to the recent crisis in Argentina and its effects on other Latin American countries.

continuation Refers to an extension of the trend. The trend continues to have momentum, and hence it moves onward without reversal.

contract (unit or lot) The standard trading unit on certain exchanges. A standard lot in the forex market is 100,000 units of currency. In the larger institutional interbank market a standard lot is one million units of currency.

convertible currency Currencies that can be exchanged for other currencies or gold.

correction A partial reversal of trend to correct a potentially overbought or oversold condition.

cost of carry When an investor borrows money to sustain a position. For example, a cost of carry for an investor short the NZD/USD pair at the end of 2005 would accrue to 7.25 percent annually on a cash-on-cash basis.

counterparty A participant, either a person or an institution, involved in one side of a financial transaction. With such transaction there is an associated risk (counterparty risk) that the counterparty will not be able to meet the terms outlined in the contract. This risk is usually default risk.

country risk   The risk that a government might default on its financial commitments/contracts, which typically brings serious harm to capital markets of that country, creating massive depreciation of assets.

cover on a bounce   A recommendation to exit trades on a bounce out of a support level.

cover on approach   A recommendation to exit trades for profit on approach to a support level.

credit checking   The process of verifying the creditworthiness of the counterparty. Before making a large financial transaction, it is imperative to check whether the counterparty has enough available credit to carry out/honor said transaction.

credit netting   Agreements that are made to avoid having to continually recheck credit, usually established between large banks and trading institutions.

cross rate   The exchange rate between two countries' currencies. Cross rates usually refer to pairs quoted that do not include the domestic currency. For example, in the United States, the EUR/JPY rate would be called a cross rate.

cup with handle   A chart pattern that resembles the formation of a cup and handle and offers insight into where a bullish trend can begin. Once the pattern begins to curve upward and reaches the cup line, the asset is believed to have bullish tone and be set for a rise.

currency   Notes and coins issued by the central bank or government, serving as legal tender for trade.

currency (exchange rate) risk   Risk associated with drastic changes/fluctuations in exchange rates in which one could incur a major loss.

daily charts   Charts that encapsulate the daily price movement for the currency pair traded. Since the currency market operates 24 hours a day, the daily chart typically runs from 5 P.M. New York time to the same time on the following day.

day trading   Refers to the process of entering and closing out trades within the same day or trading session.

dealer   One who acts as a principal in the transaction and accepts the order to buy or sell. A dealer differs from an agent in that he takes ownership of the asset, and thereby is exposed to market risk.

deficit   An excess of liabilities over assets, of losses over profits, or of expenditure over income.

delivery   The exchange by both parties (buyer and seller) of the traded currency.

deposit   Refers to the process of borrowing and lending money. The deposit rate is the rate at which money can be borrowed or lent.

depreciation   The decline in the value of an asset or a currency.

derivative   A security derived from another and whose value is dependent on the underlying security from which it is derived. Examples of derivatives are future contracts, forward contracts, and options. Underlying securities can include stocks, bonds, or currencies. Derivatives can be very actively traded, often in greater volume than the underlying asset, and are usually used to hedge portfolio risk.

descending triangle   A bearish continuation pattern indicating distribution consisting of two or more comparable lows forming a horizontal line at the bottom. Descending triangles are bearish patterns that indicate distribution. The definitive bearish signal of a descending triangle is when support on the lower edge of the triangle is broken.

devaluation   When the value of a currency is lowered against another (i.e., it takes more units of the domestic currency to purchase a foreign currency). This differs from depreciation in that depreciation occurs through changes in demand in the foreign exchange market, whereas devaluation typically arises from direct government policy. A currency is usually devalued to improve the country's balance of trade, so that its exports become cheaper for the rest of the world and imports more expensive to domestic consumers.

dirty float (managed float)   An exchange rate system in which the currency is not pegged, but is managed by the central bank to prevent extreme fluctuations in the exchange rate. The exchange rate is managed through changes in the interest rate to attract/detract capital flows or through the buying and selling of the currency. This system is contrasted with a pure float.

double top and bottom   A pattern that implies an upper limit—the top—and lower limit—the bottom—that the currency pair has touched twice but has failed to penetrate. Accordingly, the asset can be expected to meet resistance or find support at those price levels.

Dow Theory   One of the first technical analysis ideas, the Dow Theory holds that all major trends can be subdivided into three phases: entrance, whereby savvy market participants enter the market; acceleration, whereby a slew of additional participants see the trend and enter the market, thereby accelerating the trend; and consolidation, a period characterized by the initial participants exiting their trades.

economic exposure   When the cash flow of a country is vulnerable to changes in the exchange rate.

economic indicator   An economic statistic used to indicate the overall health of an economy, such as gross domestic product (GDP), unemployment rates, and trade balances. Used in fundamental analysis of foreign exchange markets to speculate on the direction of an exchange rate.

efficient markets   Markets where assets are traded at prices that are reflective of all current and relevant information.

Efficient Market Theory   The theory that the current market price reflects all information and expectations regarding the asset in question. The theory also assumes that the market cannot overprice or underprice an asset such as a currency pair, and hence the current price is the correct valuation at the time.

Elliott Wave Theory   A theory based on the notion that the market moves in waves consisting of trends followed by partial corrections. The Elliott Wave Theory states that there are five waves within an overall trend with each wave experiencing three corrections.

end of the day (mark to market)   Accounting measure, referring to the way traders record their positions, in which the value of an asset is recorded at the end of each trading day at the prevailing market price at the time. Another way that a trader can record his positions is to use the accrual system, in which only cash flows from closed-out trades are recorded.

envelopes   While Bollinger bands place boundary lines based on standard deviation, envelopes place lines at fixed percentage points above and below a moving average line. The upper and lower limits specify entry and exit points for traders.

equilibrium A price region that suggests a balance between demand and supply for a currency pair in the marketplace.

euro The monetary unit of the European Monetary Union (EMU) used by 12 countries in the European Union. It is now the legal tender in Germany, France, Belgium, the Netherlands, Luxembourg, Spain, Portugal, Italy, Austria, Ireland, Finland, and Greece.

European Central Bank The central bank of the EMU, responsible for the monetary policy of all member countries.

European Monetary Union (EMU) An institution of the European Union (EU), whose primary goal is to establish a single currency (the euro) for the entire EU.

exponential moving average (EMA) While the simple moving average distributes weight equally across the data series, exponentially weighted moving averages give greater weight to more recent data.

Federal Deposit Insurance Corporation (FDIC) A regulatory agency of the United States created to oversee that bank deposits are insured against bank failures. It was created in 1933 to restore confidence in the banking system. It insures up to U.S. $100,000 per banking institution.

Federal Reserve/Fed The central bank of the United States, responsible for monetary policy of the country.

Fibonacci numbers Derived from a sequence of numbers in which each successive number is the sum of the two previous numbers, Fibonacci numbers quickly dovetail to stable ratios. These Fibonacci ratios are used frequently in the FX market to project possible price retracement and extension levels or recent moves.

fixed exchange rate When the exchange rate of a currency is not allowed to fluctuate against another (i.e., the exchange rate remains constant). Typically, under fixed exchange rate regimes, currencies are allowed to fluctuate within a small margin. Fixed exchange rate regimes require central bank intervention to maintain the fixed rate.

fixed interest rate An interest rate used for loans, mortgages, and bonds that remains constant throughout the period of the loan.

flag/pennant A flag or pennant formation is characterized by a quick price thrust followed by a period of consolidation. It is considered a continuation pattern with price expected to follow through in the direction of the original thrust.

flat on a failure   A recommendation to take profits on a long trade if the rate tests but fails to break the specified level.

flat/square   To have either no positions or positions that cancel each other out.

floating interest rate   An interest rate that is allowed to adjust with the market. The opposite of a fixed interest rate.

foreign currency effect   Refers to how changes in the exchange rate affect the return on foreign investments such as stocks or bonds.

foreign exchange (FX, forex)   The buying and selling of currencies.

forward contract   A deal in which the price for the future delivery of a commodity is set in advance. The forward rate is obtained by adding the margin to the spot rate. It is used to hedge against adverse fluctuations in the exchange rate that can affect the amount of profit or loss at that future date.

forward points   Refers to the pips that were added to or subtracted from the current exchange rate to obtain the forward price/rate.

forward rate agreement (FRA)   An agreement that allows for borrowing and lending at a constant interest rate for a specified period in the future.

front office   Refers to the sales personnel (trading and other business personnel) in a financial company.

fundamental analysis   The analysis of economic indicators and political and current events that could affect the future direction of financial markets. In the foreign exchange market, fundamental analysis is based primarily on macroeconomic events.

futures (financial futures)   Future contracts that commit both sides to an exchange/transaction of financial instruments, currencies, or commodities at a future date and a predetermined price. Future contracts are similar to forward contacts, but have uniform size and settlement dates and are traded on central exchanges rather than over-the-counter.

good till canceled (GTC) Refers to an order given by an investor to a dealer to buy or sell a security at a fixed price that is considered good until the investor cancels it.

head and shoulders pattern A pattern resembling two peaks (the shoulders) with a higher peak between the two shoulders (the head). The neckline, or the bottom boundary that both shoulders reach, is regarded as a key point traders can use to enter/exit positions.

hedge/hedging Strategy to reduce the risk of adverse price movements on one's portfolio and to protect against the volatility of the market. Hedging typically involves selling or buying at the forward price or taking a position in a related security. Hedging becomes more prevalent with increased uncertainty about current market conditions.

high/low Refers to the daily traded high and low price.

historical volatility A measure of the change in price over a specified time frame. Higher volatility suggests that the asset is more likely to trade within a wider range, while reduced volatility suggests the asset will trade in a tighter range.

inflation Refers to the increase in prices (price level) over time that decreases the purchasing power of the consumer. It is calculated from changes in the price index, usually a consumer price index or a GDP deflator.

initial margin The percentage of the price of a security that is required for the initial deposit to enter into a position. The Federal Reserve Board requires a minimum of 50 percent initial margin. For futures contracts, the market determines the initial margin. Typically in futures markets the margin is set at 5 percent. In currencies standard margin is set at 1 percent.

interbank rate The dealing rate at which the major banks (UBS, Deutsche Bank, Citibank, Bank of Tokyo) trade in foreign exchange.

interest parity Theory that says that the difference in interest rates across countries should be equal to the difference between the forward rate and the spot rate.

interest-rate swap Interest-rate swaps are often used by companies to reallocate their exposure to interest-rate fluctuations, typically by exchanging fixed-rate obligations for floating-rate obligations.

interest-rate swap points Refers to the basis point differential between the swap rate and some reference point, usually Treasury yields.

intermarket analysis An analysis of an underlying asset that incorporates the interrelationship of various markets—typically currencies, commodities, stocks, and bonds. Intermarket analysis is centered on the idea that the four markets are correlated.

International Swaps and Derivatives Association (ISDA) Organization defining the terms and conditions for trade in derivatives.

kiwi Term for New Zealand dollar.

leading economic indicators Such statistics as unemployment rates, consumer price index, federal funds rate, retail sales, personal income, discount rate, and the prime rate that are used to predict economic activity.

LIBOR. *See* **London Interbank Offered Rate**.

LIFFE. *See* **London International Financial Futures Exchange**.

limit order An order with restrictions on the maximum price to be paid or the minimum price to be received. As an example, if the current price of USD/JPY is 120.00/05, then a limit order to buy USD 119.80 would mean that the trader would receive an execution at 119.80 or better if prices traded down that far.

liquid and illiquid markets A liquid market is one in which changes in supply and demand have little impact on the asset's price. It is characterized by many bids, offers, and players/traders; low volatility; and tight spreads. Illiquid markets have fewer players, larger spreads, and usually less volume.

liquid assets Those assets, usually short-dated assets like Treasury bills, that can easily be turned into money.

liquidation The process of closing out long or short positions by offsetting transactions. Also refers to the process of selling all assets of a bankrupt company to pay off first creditors and then shareholders.

liquidity The ability of a market to absorb large transactions with minimal to no impact on price.

London Interbank Offered Rate (LIBOR)   The rate at which major international banks lend to one another. It is widely used as the benchmark for short-term interest rates.

London International Financial Futures Exchange (LIFFE)   Exchange made up of the three largest futures exchanges in the United Kingdom.

long (position)   Refers to the ownership of securities, commodities, or currencies.

loonie   Term for Canadian dollar.

MACD.   *See* **moving average convergence/divergence**.

margin   A percentage of the total value of a transaction that a trader is required to deposit as collateral. Buying on margin refers to investing with borrowed funds, and the margin requirement serves essentially as good faith deposit.

margin call   A call by a broker or dealer to raise the margin requirement of an account by seeking additional funds for deposit. The call is typically made after one or more securities have significantly declined in value.

market maker   A broker-dealer firm that trades a particular financial instrument and is willing to buy and sell at the quoted bid and ask prices. The firm lists buy and sell prices to attract customers.

market order   An order to buy or sell at the best price available in the market at present.

market risk   The risk associated with investing in the market that has not been hedged through other instruments.

maturity   The date that the security is due to be redeemed or repaid.

mine and yours   Terms used to signal when a trader wants to buy (mine) and sell (yours). As in, "Mine at 03," meaning that a trader is buying EUR/USD at 1.2003, or "Yours at 00," meaning that the trader is selling at 1.2000.

momentum   The term has two meanings: (1) a trading style by which traders go with the direction of the current trend; and (2) a technical indicator that measures the rate of change of an asset over a given time frame.

money market   Highly liquid markets for short-term investing in monetary instruments and debts, typically maturing in less than one year. Because of relatively small yields due to the short-term nature of the instruments, transactions occur in large amounts and thus participants are mainly banks and other large financial institutions.

moving average   An average of a number of specified historical time periods from the point on the chart. Moving averages offer an indication of the clear direction and slope of the trend in the market.

moving average convergence/divergence (MACD)   The MACD indicator relies on plotting the difference between two moving average lines—typically 12- and 26-day EMAs—as well as a signal line, which is usually the 9-day EMA of the MACD itself. If the signal line—the line used to denote the rate of change—is sloping upward, this suggests that momentum is bullish; if downward, the indication is that momentum is bearish.

negative or bearish divergence   Occurs when two or more indicators or chart patterns do not yield the same analysis as price direction.

net worth   The difference between the values of assets and liabilities. For public companies this is referred to as shareholder's equity.

off-balance sheet   Refers to financing or the raising of money by a company that does not appear on the company's balance sheet, such as interest-rate swaps and forward rate agreements.

offer   The price (or rate) at which a seller is willing to sell.

offsetting transaction   When a trader enters an equivalent but opposite position to an already existing position, thereby balancing his positions. An offsetting transaction to an initial purchase would be a sale.

one cancels other order (OCO order)   An if-then order that cancels the other part of the same order once it is executed. An OCO order for a long EUR/USD position at 1.2000 with 1.2100 limit sell and 1.1900 stop would cancel the 1.1900 stop if the 1.2100 limit exit was executed, and vice versa.

open order   An order to buy or sell that remains valid until it is executed or canceled by the customer. An order that is executed when the price of a share or currency reaches a predetermined price.

options   Tradable contracts giving the right, but not the obligation, to buy or sell commodities, securities, or currencies at a future date and at a prearranged price. Options are used to hedge against adverse price movements or to speculate against price rises or falls.

order   An instruction by a customer to a broker/dealer to buy or sell at a certain price or market price. The order remains valid until executed or canceled by the customer.

overbought   A term used to characterize a market in which asset prices have risen at a pace that is above typical market acceleration, and hence may be due for a retracement.

overnight   A position that remains open until the start of the next business day.

oversold   The opposite of overbought; exists when the price of a market declines at an abnormally fast rate, and hence is due for an upward reversal.

over-the-counter market   A market not regulated by a central exchange such as the New York Stock Exchange or the Chicago Mercantile Exchange. The spot forex market is an example of an over-the-counter market.

parabolic stop and reversal (SAR)   Best used in trending markets, parabolic SAR specifies where traders should place their stops. If parabolic SAR is above the market rate, the recommendation is to short; if it is below, the recommendation is to go long.

pegging   When a country fixes the exchange rate to another country's currency, usually to achieve price stability. Most countries that peg their currencies do so against the U.S. dollar or the euro.

pip   Standing for percentage in point, a pip is the smallest amount an exchange rate can move, typically 0.0001.

point and figure (P&F)   Unlike conventional bar, candlestick, and line charts, point and figure charts completely disregard the passage of time, opting to display only changes in prices.

political business cycle   A theory that explains changes in the economy as a result of political tactics before and after elections. Politicians will often expand the economy prior to elections to gain voter support, and implement reforms just after the elections to avoid punishment by the polity.

political risk   Risk that changes in government policies will negatively impact an investor. Political risk is especially prevalent in emerging growth markets without a long history of political stability.

position   The amount of currency or security owned or owed by an investor.

premium   The amount added to the spot price of a currency to get the forward or future price.

price transparency   Refers to the degree of access to information regarding bids and offers and respective prices. Ideally, every investor/trader would have equal access to all information in the marketplace.

pure float   An exchange rate system in which there is no central bank intervention and the exchange rate is entirely determined by the market and speculation.

quote   The offer price of a security.

rate   The price of one currency in terms of another (exchange rate).

realized and unrealized profit   Realized profits are made from the cashing in of profitable positions, while an unrealized profit is a gain from an increase in the price of an asset that has not yet been cashed in.

rectangle   Similar to the consolidation portion of a flag pattern, a rectangle is a continuation pattern denoting a trading range characterized by strong support and resistance lines. Unsurprisingly, rectangles are often known as trading ranges, consolidation zones, or congestion areas.

Relative Strength Index (RSI)   An oscillator that measures the size of recent upward trends against the size of downward trends within the specified time frame. High RSI scores—above 70 or perhaps 80—indicate that the currency is oversold, and hence due for a reversal. Alternatively, low RSI scores indicate that the currency is overbought, and hence due for a fall in price.

repurchase (repo)   Involves the sales of securities now for cash with the promise made by the borrower to the lender of repurchasing those securities later at the implicit interest rate known as the repo rate. Thus a repo agreement is a *temporary* transaction in the money market. *Any* security can be used in a repo; so Treasury or government bills, corporate and Treasury/government bonds, and stocks/shares may all be used as securities involved in a repo.

resistance   A price level that a currency pair has had trouble breaking through, and hence consolidation is expected. If the resistance line holds and the currency pair retraces, the sellers have outnumbered the buyers; on the other hand, buyers have outnumbered sellers if the resistance level is broken, and price may continue higher as a new trend tries to establish itself.

retracements   Denotes a temporary reversal in the overall trend of the market to accommodate excessive acceleration or deceleration of asset price movement. Synonymous with **correction**.

revaluation   An increase in the exchange rate for a currency as a result of central bank intervention. Opposite of **devaluation**.

revaluation rates   Generally, in the FX market, the revaluation rates are market rates at 5 P.M. EST. Any profit or loss is marked to the market and the trader will start the next day with the position valued at the prior day's closing rate.

reversal   A pattern that suggests a potential shift or deceleration of the current trend. A reversal of an up move will be reflected in a downward price movement.

risks   Uncertainty in the possible outcomes of an action (i.e., possible returns on an investment). Risk is most commonly measured from the variance of possible outcomes. Higher risks are associated with higher rates of return, in order to induce investment in riskier ventures.

risk capital   The capital that an investor does not need to maintain his/her living standard.

risk management   Strategies and tactics the trader employs to avoid substantial risks to his portfolio.

rollover   Rolling forward to another date the value of the position and in the process accounting for the interest rate differential of the two currencies. In the FX market rollover interest is paid daily 365 days per year. Because settlement is two days forward, on Wednesdays the rollover interest is accrued for three days to account for the weekend.

rounding top and bottom   Similar to a cup with handle pattern, a rounding top signifies a rounded resistance line and a bearish overall trend. Alternatively, a rounding bottom is a bullish pattern for which the bottom curve can serve as a support line. Both patterns are best suited to longer-term analyses.

RSI. *See* **Relative Strength Index**.

settlement   The actual finalization of a contract in which the goods, securities, or currencies are paid for or delivered and the transaction is entered in the books.

short position   The selling of a borrowed security, commodity, or currency. Traders sell when they expect prices to fall.

spike (high or low)   A significantly lower low or higher high within a data series. Points where a currency spikes often signify a potential reversal in the direction of the trend, and hence can be valuable tools in analyzing a chart.

spot market   A market in which commodities, securities, or currencies are immediately delivered.

spot price   The current market price.

spread   The difference between the bid and offer price that is offered by a market maker.

sterling   Refers to the UK currency, the pound.

stochastics   Like RSI, stochastics are a momentum indicator that indicates overbought/oversold levels. High levels (above 70 or 80) are indications to enter short orders; low levels (below 30 or 20) are indications to buy. Like all oscillators, stochastics work best as a momentum indicator that measures the price of a security relative to its high/low range over a set period of time. The indicator fluctuates between 0 and 100, with readings below 20 considered oversold (bullish) and readings above 80 considered overbought (bearish).

stop order (stop-loss order)   An order used to hedge against excessive loss in which a position is liquidated at a specific prearranged price.

support   The opposite of resistance, a point on the chart where a currency pair has repeatedly held its value. When a currency pair tests support but does not break through it, buyers have outnumbered sellers; alternatively, sellers have gained control of momentum if support is broken and the currency pair continues to plunge downward.

swap   When a trader exchanges one currency for another, holding it for only a short period. Swaps are typically used to speculate on interest rate movements. Price is calculated using the interest rate differentials between the two currencies.

swap spread   The difference between the negotiated and fixed price of the swap. The size of the spread depends on market supply and participating parties' quality of credit.

swing high/low   A point on the chart that represents a relative peak or bottom in price. Technical traders often use swing highs and lows as reference points to place stop or entry orders at those levels.

Swissie   Refers to the Swiss franc.

symmetrical triangle   Also referred to as a coil, usually forms during a trend as a continuation pattern. It contains at least two lower highs and two higher lows. At the time these points are conjoined, the lines converge as they are extended and the symmetrical triangle takes shape.

technical analysis   A technique used to try to predict future movements of a security, commodity, or currency, based solely on past price movements and volume levels. It examines charts and historical performance.

tick   A minimum price movement in the futures markets.

ticker   Depicts current or recent history of a currency, usually in the form of a graph or chart.

tomorrow next (tom/next)   When a trader buys and sells a currency today for delivery tomorrow.

trade price response   This term advises that price reaction to a certain level is critical. If this level breaks, then the recommendation would be to run with the market direction (i.e., buy a break above resistance level; sell a break below a support level). However, if a price stalls at this level and is rejected, then the recommendation is to go with this also (i.e., sell at a resistance level that is tested and holds; buy at a support level).

transaction costs   The costs that are incurred by a trader when buying or selling securities, commodities, or currencies. These costs include broker commissions and spreads.

transaction date   The date a trade occurs.

trend line   A straight line drawn across a chart that indicates the overall trend for the currency pair. In an upward trend, the line is drawn underneath and acts as a support line; the opposite holds true for a downward trend. Once the currency breaks the trend line, the trend is considered to be invalid.

triple top   A pattern in which a currency has reached a price three times previously, yet has been unable to sustain movements beyond those three peaks. A triple top signifies a strong resistance level.

turnover   The number or volume of shares traded over a specific time period. The larger the turnover, the more active the market.

two-way price   A price that includes both the bid and offer price. The National Association of Securities Dealers (NASD) requires that market makers have both bid and ask prices for any security, currency, or commodity in which they make a market. This is called a two-sided market.

uptick   A price quote that is higher than the preceding quote for the same currency.

uptick rule   A regulation pertaining only to the stock market, requiring that if a security is to be traded short, the price in the trade prior to the short trade has to be lower than the price of the present short trade.

U.S. prime rate   The interest rate at which the major U.S. banks lend to major clients.

value date   The date that payment is exchanged between two parties.

variance   Measures the volatility of a data set/data points from the mean. It is calculated by adding the squares of the standard deviations from the mean and dividing by the number of data points (i.e., taking the average of the standard deviations).

variation margin   A call by a broker to increase the margin requirement of an account during a period of extreme market volatility.

volatility   The tendency of prices/variables to fluctuate over time. It is most commonly measured using the coefficient of variation (the standard deviation divided by the mean). The higher the volatility, the higher the risk involved.

volume   The number of shares or contracts traded for a certain security or on an exchange during a period. The FX market does not report volume.

weekly charts   Charts for which each candlestick or bar encapsulates data for the currency pair for the prior week.

whipsaw   Term used to describe sharp price movements and reversals in the market. An example of a whipsaw would be when shortly after a trader opens a long position the currency pair plummets and then just as quickly recovers its value.

yard   Term for a billion units of currency, as in "I am selling a yard of sterling."

Index